# LETTERS TO THE PIONEERS

This book is set in the typeface Athelas designed by Veronika Burian and Jose
Scaglione.

Paperback ISBN: 978-1-955546-82-9
Hardcover ISBN: 979-8-3481-3978-0

A Publication of *Remnant Publishing*

| 1 24 24 18 16 |

Published in the United States of America

# Letters to the
# PIONEERS

## Nate Johnston

To the bravest pioneers I know, Christy, Charlotte, Sophie, and Ava. You have known this path more than most and have taught me to stay the path even in the hardest moments and find the joy in the midst of it. You have taught me that it's not about what you do but it's who you do it for and who you pioneer with. You are all my everything and it's been an honor to take the road less travelled for Jesus with my family. Thanks for believing in my voice..

To Jen Miskov, Thankyou for meeting with me in 2020 in Redding to tell me that you believed I had a message for the pioneers. You saw it before I saw it myself. These letters are the fruition of that.

To Chris Harvey, Thankyou for pioneering more than most know you have. It was your yes to the unusual call that gave me the courage to lean fully in.

# CONTENTS

*Introduction*

# BEING SHEPHERDED BY JESUS

**pioneer** / pīə ˈnir

*One who ventures into unknown or unclaimed territory to settle.*

*One who opens up new areas of thought, research, or development.*

*A soldier who performs construction and demolition work in the field to facilitate troop movements.*

One morning in 2017, I went into a very clear vision of Jesus. He was walking in the wilderness with the wind blowing around Him and the sun beating down on Him. His face was draped in cloth to protect Himself from the elements. He seemed focused and fixed, yet He was also struggling. Then I heard a voice say, "If you are the Son of God, tell these stones to become bread." Jesus answered, "It is written: 'Man shall not live on bread alone, but on every word that comes from the mouth of God'" (see Matthew 4:3-4).

I realized that I was seeing Jesus being tempted and tested in the wilderness. I watched as He kept being bombarded on every side by the enemy with accusations, thoughts, and the temptation to bow out and leave the place of ultimate testing and torment He was in. But He persisted. It wrecked me deeply to see my Savior like this, but at that moment, I had a divine revelation: "Jesus went through this so that I didn't have to feel alone in my wilderness!"

You see, Jesus experienced everything that mankind could ever or would ever experience: the pain, crushing, wounding, heartache, sickness, affliction, and every mental battle we could ever have. Before we went through it, Jesus already did. Look at this verse below:

> *"For we do not have a high priest who is unable to empathize with our weaknesses, but we have one who has been tempted in every way, just as we are—yet he did not sin" (Hebrews 4:15).*

## JESUS: THE ULTIMATE PIONEER

After I had this encounter with Jesus, it took me back to my childhood, where I felt so alone and like no one, not even God, knew my pain. But the reality is that Jesus did know my pain and He did know what I walked through. I wasn't alone, and this simple truth shifted the way I did life, family, ministry, and kingdom. Jesus wasn't just with me; He had gone before me as my Pioneer.

> *"...fixing our eyes on Jesus, the pioneer and perfecter of faith. For the joy set before him he endured the cross, scorning its shame, and sat down at the right hand of the throne of God" (Hebrews 12:2).*

## THE PRIZE OF PIONEERING

I guess as a pioneer, I always felt like my role was to be cast off or sent out alone—because it sure did feel like that. It felt like being a pioneer would mean I would always be on the outside of the community and had to feel misunderstood and just deal with it. But what if I was missing the prize of pioneering that was right in front of me? What if I had been pioneering alone and had not involved Jesus this whole time? What if my definition of a pioneer had been wrong this whole time?

What if a pioneer was less about doing something new and simply following Jesus wherever He led us? This makes it a whole lot simpler. The activity and the doing are definitely important, but it's secondary to being surrendered, which at its core is the essence of the pioneering life. Just as Jesus surrendered to the will of the Father to go to the cross, we live surrendered to wherever God wants to lead us.

What I'm trying to introduce to you as we begin this book is the epiphany of companioning and co-laboring with Jesus on your pioneering journey. Far too many pioneers are shipwrecked because they do this calling in their own strength or they walk it out in misery and deep soul sickness because they simply didn't know they had someone in their corner. But imagine if Jesus were to send you letters along the way to encourage and support you. Imagine how you would navigate your path if you were able to hear the Father's heart for what you were walking through.

Pioneers need a shepherd. They need an intimate connection with God and the brooding of the Spirit. They need their arms lifted up and they need words of honey when they are being persecuted and slandered, and they need a drink of water when the terrain is hot and glasses when they can't see. And this is why I believe I am writing this book with the Holy Spirit: to help you stay on the path as you pioneer with Jesus.

## IT STARTED WITH A SENTENCE

But before I go any further (and with all that in mind), I want to share how this book concept came about. On January 10th, 2023, I was flying with my family from Australia to Dallas, Texas, after a four-year season of hard pioneering on many fronts. So much so that we dreaded this flight in the fear that we were again leading our family into greater instability and unknowns for the sake of the kingdom. We had so much warfare for a year before returning:

bogus words from people telling us we had missed God and many "Joseph's brothers" trying to get us to forfeit the calling.

So as the plane lights were dimmed and everyone was asleep in the middle of this 16-hour flight, I was extremely agitated, and my soul was disturbed within me. "Had I missed it? Was I doing the wrong thing?" I asked myself. My heart was sunk and I felt like I was in the garden of Gethsemane, crushed and broken before the Lord. Then He spoke: "Thank you for your yes, Nate."

That was it... One sentence that calmed the storm in me. At that moment, I knew He had led us here. Then He told me to start writing what He was going to give me. In the next hour, I wrote this title, the outline of 30 chapters, and a few chapters themselves. It just flooded out.

So that leads us to this moment. You are here because you are not just longing for encouragement as a pioneer but also to feel shepherded by the Lord on your journey in a way you haven't known.

I believe on this journey that God is going to make you feel known, covered, and shepherded so that your days ahead as a pioneer are your best days and that you finish your race well.

Let's begin!

*"Enter by the narrow gate; for wide is the gate and broad is the way that leads to destruction, and there are many who go in by it. Because narrow is the gate and difficult is the way which leads to life, and there are few who find it." (Matthew 7:13-14)*

# IT STARTS WITH DISCONTENT

*Pioneer, Pioneer*
*Keep pressing onwards beyond your fears*
*Only your Father goes before you to your own frontier*
*You're a Pioneer. —Rick Pino*

*Dear Pioneers,*

It starts with discontent. It starts with a sudden discomfort, dissatisfaction, frustration, and feeling like something is off or missing. It starts with a deep crying out to deep, a longing for more.

It starts with a grief that sits in the very recess of your soul that is telling you that something is out of alignment, and you need to pay attention to whatever it is or you'll keep feeling this sorrow overtake you.

It's the epiphany of the vast unknown that needs to be explored and the incredible discontent that you have with your current surroundings.

It's the realization that unless you move, shift, and break out of where you are, you'll no longer be fulfilling the call of God upon your life in the way that you are meant to.

## DAVID'S DISCONTENT

I believe David lived with the same discontent. A boy whose sole job was to shepherd sheep in the wilderness. A boy who was overlooked, unseen, invisible, and outside the system. When Samuel came to the house of Jesse to look for a king, he was so overlooked that even his father said, "These are all my sons," and David was not one of them. Yet God saw him. When David was anointed by Samuel, it's like he was suddenly commissioned with a holy discontent that would lead him out of his season of minding sheep and into a season of stepping into the greater calling upon his life.

I believe this discontent is what caused David to see Goliath not as a problem or an obstacle or a mountain in front of him, but as an opportunity.

David saw Goliath as his responsibility to take care of because he was driven by a discontent that was not his own, but the Lord's. He knew that this Goliath had his name on it, and unless he took this Goliath down, he just wouldn't be fulfilling the call that was upon his life and would be falling into disobedience.

He knew this giant was made for him and him alone, even though by outward appearances, he was unqualified, not equipped, too small, and didn't have the right armor. Yet against all odds, this discontent was what drove him into his destiny and secured the victory for his people.

So many times, we've felt this over the years, and I believe many men and women of God, leaders, and pastors around the world have felt the same discontent, too. But we have seen it as a sin, saying, "There's something wrong with me. I must be ungrateful. There must be something wrong with my heart. I better ask for forgiveness. I better repent!"

But what if God placed that upon your life to shift you out of the stagnancy you've been in and used it to lead you into something you didn't even know you were created for?

This discontent is not the fruit of a heart that is complacent, but a life that is surrendered.

This discontent is the sign and the symptom of a person who has said yes to the Lord, and God has said, "Okay, here is your next assignment, but it's going to be uncomfortable. Here is your next assignment, but you are going to move against the grain. Here is your next assignment, but you're going to have to forsake all to follow it. It's gonna cost you everything."

## THE TEARING OF DIFFERENT CLOTHS

It could be said that this discontent feels like a tearing away. It feels like God is literally detaching you from every place of comfort or area you placed your trust in that was shakeable or sinking sand.

It's a sovereign act of the Lord to begin to close doors and lead you out of things that would only cause you to be stuck or stagnant and tethered to the old move and the old thing. And right now, God is shaking up the church, and He's making us feel a discontent for what no longer carries His glory.

He's making us feel a dissatisfaction to keep eating the old manna of yesterday. We can't keep reheating the old moves frozen meals. We can't keep snacking on the party food of the kingdom of God when we're called to hunt and find the meat, the new thing that God is doing.

We can't keep licking the last drops of the old wine when we're called to tap into the new and usher it into the earth.

Ever heard the phrase, "You are made from a different cloth"? Pioneer, that is you. You are literally fashioned in heaven with a DNA and language for a time yet to come.

*"No one sews a patch of unshrunk cloth on an old garment, for the patch will pull away from the garment, making the tear worse. Neither do people pour new wine into old wineskins. If*

*they do, the skins will burst; the wine will run out and the wine-skins will be ruined. No, they pour new wine into new wineskins, and both are preserved" (Matthew 9:16-17).*

Recognize in this moment that you are not a rebel. You are not against the church. You just don't fit that mold. You don't fit the old thing because you're called to usher in the new.

You are no longer fed by something that no longer carries the fullness of glory because you are called to tap into the unlimited flow of a new spring bursting up.

## THE TEARING AWAY OF THE FAMILIAR

Pioneers, this is a time that you are feeling the tearing taking place right now in assignments, relationships, and alignments, where God is literally causing you to feel the tearing of wineskins and bringing you into a season of having to choose to keep going along with the old or to lean into the new and be a prototype for it. It is a call to stay fruitless or be the firstfruits of the new thing.

It's a call to move away from the familiar and tried path and to lean into the unfamiliar and that which has not been walked or road-tested. It's a road few say yes to easily. But this is the hour.

It's a time when it'll be unpopular to move with the Holy Spirit, but you know that you will just not feel like you are being your authentic self unless you do.

It's a time that you may feel that tearing is taking place with some that you have been in alignment with, and you'll have to just lean into the Lord even deeper as you say yes to that process.

It's a time when you'll have to lay down those assignments that you've been running with for a long time and step into the new. And it's a time of surrendering to the new blueprints, themes, and plans that the Lord is revealing to you.

## A NEW CYCLE OF PIONEERING

I believe we're in a new cycle of pioneering, which always starts with this great discontent and holy fear. It's like where you feel a red light or a caution, or a holdback or momentary stop sign. There's just this moment of reverential warning that you cannot move forward without Him.

Like Moses said, "Unless Your glory goes before me, I will not go." In your spirit, you've just been sensing this reverential fear and this cry deep within you of, "Lord, unless Your glory goes before me, I'm done with what I have been putting my hand to" (see Exodus 33:15).

Like Elisha, who knew he couldn't go back after Elijah threw his mantle on him, you know that you just can't go back to the old plow and old activity you were involved in.

You know that your name has to be changed and your role has changed, and you have to let go of what you were doing to embrace whatever is coming.

## THE CALL TO THE PURE THING

The discontent is a call to purity because pioneers have a calling to that which is genuine, untainted, and uncompromised. The Lord uses pioneers to experience and encounter this first, so then they can lead the church out of stagnation and into that which is fresh, flowing, and pure.

Right now across the body of Christ, God is stirring up discontent in the hearts of pioneers and a remnant that have not bowed their knee to culture and have not allowed themselves to fall prey to the appetites of this world.

God is right now stirring up discontent in those within the institution who cannot be lulled to sleep like others around them, nor are they impressed by the achievements and accolades of man that are valued in the Western church. They just can't be like others who have fallen into apathy and weariness in their faith.

They just can't be sold for celebrity status or the praises of man.

God is stirring up discontent in a people that would break the church free from her chains of bondage and lead her into her next chapter and her best days.

This is why you are feeling what you are feeling right now. This is why you've been feeling unsettled with the current state of the church. Why you can't seem to even sit through a service the way you once did.

It's why you've been frustrated with the buzzwords and the cliches. You can't go back. You can't go back to the Christianity you once knew.

Pioneers, there's nothing wrong with you. You are the bell ringers of a new day and new hour in the body of Christ.

## THE GREAT DETOUR

God is right now leading you away from movements that are no longer moving. He's leading you away from messages that no longer carry the freedom they once did. And He's leading you away from the path that is going to cause you to fall asleep like the many others who have fallen asleep before their time.

He is putting a bad taste in your mouth for the ministry machine and the career Christianity model. He is breaking your longing to be seen and popular. He is, instead, giving you a voice and influence that transcends the status of man.

You are in a detour that is reshaping your affections and desires. You will find that you can no longer feel the synergy and peace you once did for Christian activities and projects you once held dear, but you'll sense the pulling away to build that which has not been done before.

Right now, God is also awakening those who have been in a season of decommissioning, a season of being on the sidelines; those that people counted as the fallen; the compromised; those who crashed and burned and shipwrecked. God is awakening them as His remnant, as His pioneers. You'll feel as if overnight, you woke up to a fresh wind and a fresh fire burning in your spirit, and the longing to break free at all costs for whatever lay ahead of you.

## CANA & THE VOID

Pioneers, just as in the story of Jesus at Cana, where the wine that was used for the feast ran out, we are in that moment right now in the body of Christ. Can you see it around you?

Can you see the evidence of the drought that has been upon the church, where people are scrambling for the last drops of an old way?

There's been a desperation, a struggle, a fight, and a wrestle.

People are desperately trying to grasp onto the memories of something powerful, yet past. Movements that have become monuments and museums, void of anything living, and a power that is no longer present.

We have traded the Holy Spirit for intellectualism. We've begun to be opinion-fueled protestors instead of powerfully-postured revivalists carrying the torch of truth and justice. We have begun to rely on our own understanding.

These are all the signs of the void, the tearing, and the crossover, and you pioneers are called to usher in the new, to be the new, to lean into the new.

The Lord today wants to affirm that what you've been feeling is not rebellion, but it is holy. This detour is Him leading you on a new pilgrimage with Him. This longing is a sign of being marked for a move that has not yet even begun.

It is a calling and a branding of a people that have been assigned to the future, and right now, they have been given the task of walking out a journey so that others can follow in it.

## THE VALLEY OF DECISION

Pioneers, right now, you are in a valley of decision, and before you are two choices: Will you choose to lean into this discontent, or will you run from it?

Will you surrender your heart to the Lord afresh?

Will you lay down your methods, your blueprints, everything you thought you knew? Will you lay them down today?

Will you say, "Yes, Jesus, I choose You over my denomination. I choose You over my theology. I choose You over the opinions of man, over the teachings of man. I choose You even above being accepted by my community, above the people I'm trying to stay connected to, above my reputation"?

Will you choose Him above all else?

Will you stop fighting the discontent and begin to step into it so that you can see the fruit of it?

We're in the void and the hallway of eras, and this is the moment not to hide and wait for it to pass, but to grasp it with both your hands and choose this moment to give your life and to follow Him wherever it leads.

**Pioneers, this is your brand new day and the first step on a new adventure with God. Will you say yes? Only time will tell.**

*Letter Two*

# BURNING THE PLOW

*Dear Pioneers,*

When you first begin your journey of pioneering, you'll begin with a season of the deepest surrender that you'll ever know.

It'll be a season of it costing you everything just to step into your shoes as a pioneer. It will first cost you your old mindsets, methods, and ways of thinking. Then it will cost you your previous assignments, your previous alignments, and the infrastructure that you have built your life around.

You'll go through a season where it feels like everything that is shakeable will be shaken, and where it feels like everything that you had found—your identity, your purpose, your value—is removed from you for a season so that God can completely usher you into your season of effective pioneering.

Before you can launch into your season of building and walking in the lifestyle of a pioneer, you'll need your Elisha moment, and I call this the season of the burning of the plow.

In 2 Kings 19:19, Elijah threw his mantle around Elisha to call him into the ministry, and what Elisha did next was his response of surrender and yes to the call:

> *"So Elisha turned back from him, and took a yoke of oxen and slaughtered them and boiled their flesh, using the oxen's equipment, and gave it to the people, and they ate. Then he arose and followed Elijah, and became his servant" (2 Kings 19:21).*

You don't choose to be a pioneer or remnant; it's something that just happens to you as God throws Himself like a mantle around you and clothes you and anoints you for the next season. The burning of the plow is what readies us for that assignment.

## THE TWO FIRES

When God calls you to pioneer, you face two initial fires. The first refiner's fire is a result of God mantling you, where in that process, it begins to highlight and illuminate the wrong mantles, the wrong mindsets, and the wrong methods that you are operating in.

It's the refiner's fire that exposes that which is outdated, expired, and no longer conducive to your calling.

I like to call this the refiner's fire to RECEIVE. You receive your new mantle, but you also receive a new way of thinking and new mindsets. These mindsets begin to overtake your life until you reach a point where you can no longer operate or live satisfied with what you are doing or your current activity.

It's where you begin to look around you and realize that unless you step into this new mantle completely, you'll never feel fully effective in the calling on your life or fully obedient to the voice of the Lord.

The second fire is when we see Elisha burn his plow and cook the oxen. The second refiner's fire is what I like to call the refiner's fire to CONCEIVE.

It's a fire that brings you into a season of actually conceiving that which you received in the first place.

It's the refiner's fire that brings that which God had ordained for your life into your present. It's where you begin to physically and tangibly make decisions in your life that cause the old things to die and end so that God can bring the new to your doorstep.

It's where you begin to confront the areas in your life that aren't working and begin to change them and bring closure to them.

It's where you begin to draw boundaries with people around you and begin to communicate your heart, your vision, to those who've only seen you operate in one particular type of way. And it's where you begin to step out of an old mantle, an old assignment, and burn them completely to the ground and start afresh.

## TAKING OFF THE OLD RAGS

Just as when Elijah threw his mantle around Elisha and it caused him to step into a new season and new authority and anointing, it also caused him to open his eyes.

In this process, you will begin to notice the vast disparity between the place God is leading you into and the place you've been living, and your eyes will suddenly be opened to the greatness and holy purpose that He has suddenly called you into and the place of limitation you've been living in.

It'll be a moment where you realize why you've been feeling so discontent, and that is because you've been living so far from the richness of your calling. You've been living in a place of barrenness and fruitlessness, and God had to do something drastic to pull you out of it.

I call this part of the process "The Old Rags Syndrome." It's the season where you begin to shake off the many areas that you've been living far from the place of purpose, and also step into the fullness of your identity in Christ.

It's where God begins to agitate you even further, and it leads you into a season where you have to violently cast off all of the mindsets that you had about yourself, the lies you've been believing, and the inferior and counterfeit mantles that you have been wearing for a long time.

It's where God leads you into a season of laying those things on the altar. But let me make this clear: It won't feel like you are mantled with something special at this stage in the process.

It won't feel like you've been covered. It won't feel like something new has come upon you. It will feel like you are naked. You'll feel vulnerable. You'll feel raw. You'll even feel a little bit frustrated at God because He's leading you into such a season of having to let go of so much without being privy to the fullness of what He's leading you into.

This, my pioneer friends, is what pioneering life is all about. This is the season that you'll know what it's like to make a sacrifice. This is a season where you'll wake up without directions, without a blueprint, without even knowing where to step forward, and you'll have to choose over and over again to keep saying yes, surrendering all your questions, and leaning into the place of His presence so that He can lead you into your next day and next chapter.

## COOKING THE OXEN

Pioneers, one of the hardest parts in this process is having to practically let go of the old assignments that have felt like a child to you.

It's the assignments and roles you have given your life to for maybe two, three, five, ten, or 20 years, and suddenly the Lord will ask you to give them to Him. You know you need to do it, but it'll feel like you are laying down something that you've given your life for and trading it for something that feels like sinking sand in the moment.

Be aware, people around you won't understand. They will not be able to comprehend why you're making such a foolish decision. They'll come to you with their counsel and their advice, and much of it will feel like wisdom. Much of it will make sense to you in the natural.

You'll agree with them. "You're right, I'm doing something that looks silly. I'm doing something that does not make sense." Yet, everything on the inside of you will know, "This is where the Lord is leading me. This is where the Spirit of God is taking me, and I can't trade it for anything else!"

It's a season where you'll look like you are forfeiting your birthright for the sake of something that is a wind, something that is fleeting. People will try to talk you out of it, but it is your responsibility in this time to keep laying down the words and even good counsel of those around you and lean into the voice of the Lord.

His voice will need to be the loudest one in this season. Will you continue to follow Him? Will you continue to say yes to His leading even when the masses around you are calling you crazy? This is the greatest test.

This part of the process as a pioneer is the first make or break. This is the place that few tend to leave. It feels like it's the interview room of the pioneer. If you make it out of this place, then you will pioneer. If you don't, you'll stay in this waiting room for many years living frustrated and feeling like you have no outlet to be able to establish that which God has given you: the blueprints, the desires, and the strategies.

You'll live in this waiting room wondering why you're never fully released, and that comes down to one thing: Have you yet laid on the altar people's opinions, words, and counsel, or are you still elevating them above the voice of the Lord in your life?

I feel like the Lord is wanting to invite you to surrender those words afresh to Him. I feel like the Lord is wanting to give you an opportunity to say, "Lord, I repent for placing their counsel above the obedience to follow You, and today, above all else, I choose You."

Now watch as God begins to cause you to leave that waiting place and the holding pattern. Now watch as He begins to highlight your next steps.

## IT FIRST LOOKS LIKE DEATH

Yes, pioneers, this part of the process feels like death, and I can't paint it any other way. It's where everything that you have in your hands needs to be let go. It's where God will get you to empty your hands and your heart of everything that you once held dear. It's the season of the seeds falling to the ground and dying. It's the season of having to let go of all the expectations that you had.

It's a season where you'll look around you and see so many circumstances that didn't pan out the way you thought they would—where you didn't quite meet that goal, and you didn't quite see that dream realized. Yet, in the face of those things, the Lord will say, "Will you hand them to Me? Will you give them to Me? Will you lay them down for something I want to give you?"

It's a moment of truth for the pioneers. Are our dreams more important than He is? Are our desired outcomes more important than the closeness of His presence?

## SMASHING CEILINGS

Know that as you begin to burn the plow, you are actually stepping into a season of smashing ceilings. You'll notice that God begins shaking that which is keeping you held and that which is keeping you captive.

It's a season where your eyes will be open to see the many traps and the cement that has been placed around your feet from people, circumstances, and spiritual entities, both generationally and enacted by open doors in your life, and God will begin to shake you free from them.

The pioneering life is not a lifestyle of brassed heavens or ceilings. It is not a lifestyle of rigid control or intimidating structures. It is not a lifestyle of being hedged in, but of breaking out.

And God in this season will cause you to break free from everything that is keeping you backed into a corner and caged.

Watch as every single restraint begins to come to the surface. Watch as your eyes are open to see the many restraints around you, and He begins to lead you into confronting them, breaking them, and stepping into new realms of freedom in your life.

It's just like the scene in Willy Wonka where he takes the elevator up and it bursts through the ceiling of the building and causes them to see higher, not just above his factory but above the whole city. God has called you to break and smash ceilings in the church so that you can be the one who sees above.

He's called you to smash through the ceilings of religiosity and limited thinking that is keeping the body of Christ in bondage, and He will first lead you out of that bondage so that you can then lead them into freedom.

There are many ways that this freedom will come to you, and I would like to share a few with you.

## CLOSURE TO SPIRITUAL TIES & VOWS

One of the areas of bondage that God will cause you to confront is spiritual vows and ties. One of these is the spiritual ties to people, to places, to roles and assignments that are no longer conducive for you to walk or operate in. There may have been a grace for them in a previous season, but there is no grace for them anymore, and if you still live tied to those things, you'll be unable to operate in the fullness of the new anointing and mantle that's upon your life. You'll feel continually conflicted, you'll feel continually confused about your role and the office that you operate in, and you'll live in this place of frustration, not able to fully commit to the new unction upon your life, the new oil that is now flowing. You will try to operate in the old thing and wonder why there's no longer any fruit.

You need to break some of those spiritual ties; you need to begin to confront the areas that you are still thinking in the old way, in the old methods; and you need to begin to confront even some of the ways that you're still living in Egypt when you're meant to operate in a Canaan mindset.

This happens most effectively when we begin to confront the vows that we've created, the words that we've uttered verbally that have been tying us to some of these old assignments.

What have you said in the past? What vows have you made that are keeping you stuck?

Have you been in agreement with them? Have you been stuck in contracts and agreements with people that you can no longer fulfill because God has moved you on? Have you given your life to a leader to a person or to a ministry without God's consent or approval, and it is keeping you stuck?

Have you given your vow, your word to someone that God never asked you to? Today, begin to break the vows. Ask the Lord to highlight them to you. Begin to confront the contracts and sever them with the blood of Jesus where you have been stuck to the old things, the old ways, to people, places, and assignments that you can no longer effectively honor.

## THE ENDING OF FALSE OWNERSHIP & AGREEMENTS

As you begin to confront some of these areas, what will come to the surface right away are your alignments. You see, many of us have only known what it is like to be in contract, but we've not known what it is to be in covenant.

You see, David had a contract with Saul to take down Goliath, but he was in covenant with Jonathan, and they're two very different things.

Many of us have been in false coverings and accountabilities. Many of us have been in contracts that have kept us tied down to systems and networks and to man-made structures instead of in covenant.

One seeks to tie you down as a drone to fulfill a need within a building environment, whereas a covenant is family, and it knits hearts together for the common purpose of building the kingdom of God.

And pioneer, you are not called to be in contracts. You are called to be in covenant.

Contracts will place you in a bind that disables you from effectively walking in your calling as a pioneer. Being in contract with Saul will disable you from effectively fighting the battles you need to fight and extending the kingdom of God because you will be limited to the vision and the mission of the person you have been in contract with.

You need to break those contracts. You need to confront the areas of false covering and accountability that you have created and stepped into before you'll ever effectively be able to extend the kingdom of God. You'll constantly feel the pressure and the parameters of that Saul you've given your life to and never fully live in the abandon and the obedience to Christ that you were called to.

And many right now are facing this hurdle. They've been part of big movements, megachurches, and empires. They've given their lives to leaders that they love and look up to and admire. Even mothers and fathers in the faith, great people that may even have great motives. But if it's a contract you've entered into without the Lord's endorsement, then it will be bondage no matter who it is to, and it needs to break.

If you're feeling the conviction of the Holy Spirit right now as you read these words, then the Lord is leading you into a time of breaking the contracts you've entered into and the false ownership that's been over you. You can't operate as a pioneer with the brandings of man on your life. You can't effectively operate as a pioneer if you've been marked by a man's movements instead of the Spirit of God.

God is a jealous God, and He wants you reserved for Himself. You are His remnant. He set you aside for a purpose, and He does not want you to be under man any longer, and today, those contracts need to be torn up.

## YOU CAN'T TAKE THEM WITH YOU

Yes, make no mistake. This part of the process is a massive test that will determine whether you follow the Lord or whether you choose to stay in the comforts and confines of the past. The greatest hurdle that every pioneer faces and the greatest test is the laying down of relationships for the Lord.

Why is this such a hard thing for the body of Christ? I think it purely comes from the desire to not be alone, but it also reveals where we have idolized people and relationships above the voice of the Lord in our lives, and it is often one of the first trigger areas for a pioneer.

People around you will begin to say, "Why are you doing this? What is wrong with you? What is going on in your life? You need to stop that!"

And in that moment, you'll realize something. You'll realize you are no longer equally yoked with so many people around you. In fact, I would say that with 90% of the people around you, you'll discover in a moment that you are unequally yoked with, and you can no longer continue to walk with them in your calling as a pioneer, or at least in the capacity or the current dynamics of the relationship that you have established with them.

When you realize this, you know you will need to confront those unequally weighted yokes. You will know at that moment that you will have to begin to establish some boundaries in your life that give them the choice of whether they're going to walk alongside you and come up higher with you, or they're going to stay down where they are and effectively sever the friendship that you've created.

If this is you—whether you are either going through this or you're about to go through this—I want to say that I know it's not easy, but there is such a reward waiting on the other side of your obedience to choose God above even these friendships.

What you have to remember is that you are pioneering family and new-era relationships, and that doesn't happen by tolerating unequal yokes but by modeling better values.

You're pioneering a tribe, a group, a people, and it begins with you and it begins in this moment in the dynamics of the relationships that you have around you.

## YOU CAN'T BE THEIR FIXER & GOD'S PIONEER

The sad reality is that most will decide to stay where they are, and you have to leave them behind, knowing you can't drag them with you. You can't make them pioneers with you. You can't make them see the way you see. You can't do any of those things, and that is not your role or your calling.

As a pioneer, your calling is obedience to Christ. This is what you need to know in this part of the process because one of the first reactions or responses that we make is trying to appease people and trying to fix them.

We try to bring them with us in the hopes that they will come. We try to explain to them who we are and what God's doing in our lives while facing their lack of enthusiasm and understanding.

We do whatever it takes to try to lead them higher with us, to no avail. You are not their fixer. You are a pioneer of the Most High God.

You are not called to try to repair and fix every crack in every relationship around you. That is not your calling and that is not the destiny that is upon your life.

## CHOOSING MOMENTARY ISOLATION FOR PURIFICATION

"But won't this send me into isolation? Won't this just lead me into a place of being cut off from everyone around me?" Yes, for a season, it will feel like every single person that you once loved or held dear will be cut off from your life. It will feel like God has exiled you when really it's momentary purification for the commissioning that He's leading you into.

It's where God leads you into the chamber of His glory so that He can surround you, fill you, set you apart, brand you, and mark you for this new season. You cannot see it through the eyes of isolation. You must see it through the eyes of intimacy in being set apart. Otherwise, you will fall and you will go back to where you started.

Know in this moment—if this is where you are and you've been in a season of isolation for some time now—this is not the place that God wants you to stay. It is simply for a moment to set you apart and to brand you for something fresh. The enemy would like to keep you here, but it is not where you are meant to stay.

## THE SACRIFICE THAT'S TOO FAR

And the final straw of this process can be the most painful. And I don't want to spare you of it, but I want you to be aware. When you step out as a pioneer, don't be surprised if your family is the first to come and persecute you. Do not be surprised if they are the ones that oppose you the most in the time when you were expecting their support, expecting them to rally on God's side holding up your arms. But instead, they become your greatest protestors and discouragements of the calling of God upon your life.

If you are able to effectively establish boundaries and keep relationships with them, then well done. But in many cases, for pioneers and those called to embark on a new journey carrying the new era themes and messages of God's heart, you will face this.

And I hear the Lord saying right now, "Will you lay them down for Me? Will you stop trying to appease them and will you look at Me? Look at Me, son, look at Me. Daughter, do not look behind you. Do not look around you. Leave them to Me and entrust them to Me today. I have them in the palm of My hand!"

Now watch what He does. And for those that the Lord is asking you today to give them to Him, this is what the Word of God says:

> *"'Truly I tell you,' Jesus replied, 'no one who has left home or brothers or sisters or mother or father or children or fields for me and the gospel will fail to receive a hundred times as much in this present age: homes, brothers, sisters, mothers, children and fields—along with persecutions—and in the age to come eternal life'" (Mark 10:29-30).*

## PIONEERS MANTLED IN GLORY

I feel there are so many pioneers reading this, and this call has already cost you so much. And the Lord is simply saying to you today as you burn the plow and are obedient to make that separation, that line in the sand:

"Watch now as I fashion you and mantle you with My glory, for son, daughter, you have not seen anything yet. You're about to see the glory come upon your life in a way that you've never experienced. Now watch as, over the years to come, that which looks like stupidity and foolishness, I begin to reveal My glory through. And these foolish things that you've said yes to will confound the wise and they will soon see the fruit. And you will see the fruit as you burn the plow and step into the place of obedience to this new calling I have called you into. And you will SEE ME and you will know Me and you will no longer live wandering or wondering, but you will begin to experience the fulfillment of being clothed with Me and being a conduit of My glory in the earth!"

Wow, the pioneering life is the life of being clothed by God. That wrecks me deeply.

It doesn't always feel fair that we walk a rugged road, and it doesn't feel fair that we go through such emptying. But oh, when that mantle comes upon you, when He clothes you with His very person, there is nothing like it.

If you have not experienced that yet, soon you will, and you'll realize that in light of what He clothes you with, what you have had to let go of and give away for this calling will feel like filthy rags. It will feel like you've given Him nothing in comparison to the glory.

*"I consider that our present sufferings are not worth comparing with the glory that will be revealed in us" (Romans 8:18).*

Pioneers, the glory is coming. The morning is coming. The new dawn is dawning. Let me prophesy this. There shall be a new dawn that comes upon you. The Lord says over you today:

*"...you who have only tasted but death. You shall taste the new morning rays. You shall taste the sweetness and the honey from the rock and the sustenance in this season, for I do not ask for you to surrender without then giving something greater. I do not ask you to lay something down without then pouring out a double portion upon your life. And in this season, I am going to cause you to taste the sweetness and the fatness that shall break yokes around you as you forge the new road ahead in My name."*

# UNCOMFORTABLE MANTLES OF GLORY

*Dear Pioneers,*

It's time to pick up the mantle that only you can wear and operate.

You've been through the season of shedding the rags and the mantles that have been forcefully and oppressively placed upon you. You've been through the season of having to violently cast off things you were never meant to carry.

Just like David, who in his moment of battle could not wear the armor that Saul had given him.

You too have realized that if you had gone into battle, if you had stepped onto your path of destiny, continuing to wear the mantles and coverings of others, you would never fully and effectively take down the giants you are called to take down.

So many of us have embarked on previous journeys that have ended in shipwreck and heartache and pain. I know you're reading this now and you're asking me, "What do I do? How do I step into the right mantle if all I've known is to wear the wrong ones? How do I know this is the right mantle?"

This is how you know that the mantle you're receiving is the right one: It comes with no conditions except to be the beloved of Jesus.

It comes with no exceptions. It comes with no rules or limitations or requirements except to be a disciple of Jesus.

You've been led on this path because what you have been given is pure.

What you have been given cannot be tainted, and God has been jealously calling you out of all the wrong mantles and false coverings and accountabilities that have only squashed you.

Now, here you are on the brink of a new day. Many of you are staring at the mantle as it sits there on the ground in the dust. There's a little bit of hesitation. "Do I pick it up? What if I'm let down by it? What if it's not what I imagined it would be? What if I'm the wrong person for it right now?"

Shake off all the discouragement, shake off all the what-ifs, and pick up your mantle.

You're in a moment like Elisha. Elijah's time to leave was coming. Elisha knew that he needed a double portion to be able to accomplish the mission that was on his life. It didn't come from a place of greed or ambition.

Elisha was demanding a double portion because his assignment required the double portion of authority, power, and signs and wonders.

The discontent in this season of your life has been, "God, I need more of You."

And without you realizing it, it has come from a deep desire from your spirit man who knows that unless you are anointed with double, you'll be unable to accomplish the calling of God upon your life.

The path that you are assigned to will designate the proportionate amount of authority, favor, and blessing.

And right now, the mantle that God has given you is that very authority, favor, and power.

And God is saying to you today, step into your mantle.

Pick it up.

Put it on.

Stop hiding from it.

Stop running from it.

It's time to own the mantle that God's given you.

You can't keep comparing mantles.

You can't keep comparing your giftings.

You can't keep comparing your situations and circumstances to those around you.

It's robbing you of picking up the mantle you've been given.

It's causing you to look to the left and the right.

It's causing you to be distracted, pioneers.

You must be focused at this moment, okay?

You can't keep listening to the words of the naysayers.

You must step into your mantle.

When Elisha asked for the double portion, Elijah said to him, "If you see me when I go, you receive what you asked."

The only requirement for receiving the mantle right now is to look to Jesus.

Look to Him.

Watch Him, nothing else.

Pioneers, keep focused.

Keep fixed.

Begin to discipline your eyes.

Begin to attune your senses to Him in a new way.

Pioneers, this is the moment as you begin to pick up your mantle, dust it off, and put it on.

It's easy to feel lost.

It's easy to feel the opposite of empowered.

You feel like you're at the beginning and you don't know which way to go.

As you pick up that mantle, you'd think that you'd suddenly feel the infusion of your strength and ability, but more often than not, it feels like you're putting on a new outfit that you haven't quite fit into yet.

The fabric feels scratchy and it's just foreign.

You knew how to operate in the old mantle. You knew at least when wearing someone else's mantle what to do with it and in it.

But now in the one that God's given you that is pure and un-filled, you're having to grow into it and it's scary.

I want to encourage you: This is a moment.

You cannot move by what you feel and what you see, but simply by faith.

Elisha did something to activate the mantle upon his life, and he grabbed that cloth and he slapped the water with it, and it parted the waters.

Don't sit dormant.

Don't sit inactive just because you're afraid.

Begin to do something with what's upon your life.

Let me make this really clear: Pioneering is not always about a feeling.

It's not always those lion and lioness moments of courage and boldness and plowing a field with passion and authority.

The overwhelming majority of the time, pioneering is the discipline of getting up every single day and doing something with the authority and anointing that's upon your life.

No matter how you feel, or no matter what you see, continue to be faithful to speak what God's given you.

No matter how many people are following you, no matter what you feel is happening with what you're doing.

Let me be even more clear: You can't look at the fruit yet. Stop looking for fruit right away.

If you look for fruit right now, you're going to get discouraged and give up.

You can't look at the fruit right now.

You need to be focused on the seed when you first begin.

This is where it feels like you're underground.

This is the messy part.

This is the part where people don't see what you're building.

They don't understand what you're cultivating, and you don't, either. This is where you find it hard to believe in yourself, and you're going to have to sit at the feet of Jesus every day to give you the strength to get up and keep doing something.

Keep doing something.

You can't forfeit right now.

You can't forfeit the calling on your life and you can't forfeit the mantle that you've been given.

Let me prophesy over you, pioneer.

You have a Psalm 24 anointing, and the Lord today is commissioning you with a Psalm 24 mantle.

What is the Psalm 24 mantle?

It's the mantle of clean hands and a pure heart that causes you to ascend the hill of the Lord.

Not everyone can go there, only those with clean hands.

And you may say, "Well, I don't know if I'm clean."

If you're reading this right now, you're more set apart than you know.

If you're reading this right now, you've been through the fire and you've been through the process, and the Lord is mantling you afresh with an anointing of holiness and a raging fire. A purity that has been sifting what is pure and what is not pure from your life.

God is leading you to pioneer something that is undefiled and uncompromised from the rest of the world, and even from so much of westernized Christian culture.

Do not be afraid to ascend the mountain of the Lord and separate yourself.

Now, let me prophesy what the fruit of that will be. The fruit of this anointing and mantle will be that you'll be the gate and you'll be the door that ushers the King of glory into the earth—into your sphere and into those places where the glory is needed most.

Pioneer, you've been mantled with glory.

Now pick up your mantle and hit the water and begin your legacy today, in Jesus' name.

# THE NEW ERA SCRIBES

*Dear Pioneer,*

Have you ever watched a three-part movie that takes you through incredible highs and lows in the storyline only to end in a mysterious and inconclusive place and you have to wait for a year or more to see the sequel?

That feeling is similar to what pioneers feel when looking at the current landscape of the church and their own lives. They feel like they have seen the movie over and over but don't feel resolved that it's how the storyline should end, and if this is how you have felt, then you are right.

The problem is not only that the storyline of the church feels unfinished but also our own storylines, right?

Many have been asking, "Is this really where my book ends? Is this the greatest achievement or peak of my life? Lord, something feels unfinished and I want more adventures with You!"

So many pioneers felt at a standstill in so many ways, dealing with the delayed emotional processing from their last season, the hope deferred, tumultuous highs and lows, and the sudden cliff drop they don't know how to reconcile.

Let me speak into that by saying this: A new chapter has begun and you have been given the role of being part of writing it. Let me share a powerful vision I had years ago.

## VISION OF THE SCROLLS OF DESTINY

I was praying one night when I had a vision of the Lord opening the pages of people's books. What was first highlighted to me was that many chapters of these books were disjointed, with whole blank pages, torn pages, and pages where the sentences suddenly stopped. Secondly, I noticed that each of them had whole sections of the book where they were titled with chapters and headings but nothing was yet written.

From outward appearances, these were poorly written books, but the Lord was so invested in them as He was reading them because they were obviously highly valuable to Him.

After I saw this, I asked the Lord what I saw and what it meant, and He said to me that the books I saw were indeed the pages of people's lives, but they were actually destiny books that contained the purposes and plans of God for each one of us!

## CHAPTERS OF TRANSITION

Many people right now are in the uncomfortable chapters, where it feels like their seasons have been disjointed and don't make any sense, which is what I sensed when I saw them. It is like chapter four just doesn't seem to match chapter five and so on. In this season of transition, many have felt lost and highly confused about where they are headed, because their past season was so different from the one before them, and they are feeling visionless and in foreign territory.

The Lord said to me, "Only I can connect what needs to be connected. Only I can orchestrate what needs to be orchestrated. Where you see inconsistency and lack of direction, I have been re-directing you. I am making the chapters of your life all come together in this season as you lean into Me, trust Me, and allow Me to do what only I can do."

## THE TORN PAGES

The Lord began to speak to me about the torn pages and said to me that they represented failure and ruin that many had experienced in previous seasons but especially recently. I felt His grief as He highlighted broken marriages, loss, and disaster and ruin that had come to people and homes. There was such a brokenness that many had been so deeply torn in their hearts and overshadowed by trauma. "Come out of hiding," I hear the Father saying so tenderly. "That page of your life is not your end. Now watch Me make it your brand new beginning! I am healing your heart right now and turning the page for you where you will begin to hope again, love again, and dream again!"

As I am writing this, I am sensing that many who are reading this are being healed from rejection. I keep hearing "rejection syndrome" and see how the root of rejection keeps causing some people to be derailed in many areas once it is triggered. Those past areas where you were rejected, abandoned, and cast out are being healed right now. I command every spirit of rejection attached to you to leave right now in Jesus' name! Be restored and whole, accepted and fully loved! Father, show them Your love even as they read this.

If you felt the Holy Spirit highlighting anything to you, just take a few moments to be still in His presence and allow Him to heal you.

## THE BLANK PAGES

As I asked God about the blank pages, I heard Him say, "What looks like waiting isn't fruitless. What looks like wasting is worship." And I sensed that this represented many people who have been in a waiting season, where it has felt like they have received no steps, strategies, or direction forward and have felt stuck, frustrated, and empty and become heartsick. The Lord said, "Looks can be deceiving, because where you have surrendered to Me in the waiting, you are giving Me permission to FILL IN THE BLANKS!" In the waiting, you always end up with more than you bargained for as you keep holding on, not giving up!

## LET ME FINISH YOUR SENTENCES

I asked the Lord about the unfinished sentences that seemed to trail off as if someone had fallen asleep behind the pen. The Lord said, "Where many have grown weary and fallen asleep, I am coming to renew strength, and I will not only rejuvenate and reinstate them, but I will finish their sentences!" I sensed that the Lord was saying that this would be a season for many who had been derailed and disillusioned in the past to stand back up to their feet and see God fulfill what He promised. He is declaring over you today, "I'm not finished with you yet!"

## THE NEW PAGES OF A NEW DAY

When I asked the Lord about the new pages, I felt the presence of the Holy Spirit so strongly and then heard, "It's a new day for history to be written!" And I sensed the excitement and joy of the Lord as many wake to a brand new day in the months ahead. The months and months of the Lord bringing healing and closure to so many areas have resulted in hearts that are ready and ripe for God to embark on new adventures, clutter-free, with fresh hope and purpose for the days ahead.

It will be days of pioneering in joy and freedom without the religious shackles holding you back. It will be a new day to dream and journey with the Lord without the burdensome overheads of past seasons. It's a new day and a new beginning for many as the Holy Spirit breathes upon the pages of your life afresh. He is asking you today, "Will you allow Me to flood the pages of your life with My goodness? Will you allow Me into your heart afresh to heal, restore, and fill you? Will you leave the past behind and write the pages of history with Me?"

*"All the days ordained for me were written in your book before one of them came to be" (Psalm 139:16).*

## THE PEN, THE KEY, & THE NEW CHAPTER

In another season of asking the same questions, I had a similar vision where I was holding a pen, a key, and a book opened in the middle to a new chapter with blank pages.

I instantly knew we were shifting from one chapter into another, and there was something God wanted us to pioneer this year onward to fill those pages.

As I was thinking about this, I heard these words in my spirit: "It's up to us to write the future. We must write history!"

We aren't powerless in the storyline taking place right now. In fact, God wants us to be the writers and authors with Him of what takes place.

Pioneers, you are God's pen, and this year, He is anointing you to be His vessel of glorious poetry to usher His heart into the earth.

*"We have become his poetry, a re-created people that will fulfill the destiny he has given each of us" (Ephesians 2:10).*

In the last few years, there have been major attacks against the pioneers, the creatives, and the ones called to write history with

God through the unique expressions He has given to us all, but in this new chapter, the pages will be filled with the words, topics, themes, and language of a new day and hour.

The blank pages represent the blank slate season we are in that demands a response from the body of Christ to stand up, courageously step into the unknown, speak what has been unspoken, and create the world we want to see.

We have to close the doors to the past—the past moves, methods, ways, formulas—and embrace the uncharted road.

The key I saw is the authority God is reminding us that we have. It's the key of David, a governmental key that changes everything it locks or unlocks.

> *"I will place on his shoulder the key to the house of David; what he opens no one can shut, and what he shuts no one can open"* (Isaiah 22:22).

This speaks to me of our role to impact and change the storyline taking place in the earth and around us. We get to shut doors and open them. We get to determine what is allowed and what is not, and what is acceptable and what is not.

This new chapter slams the door to the era of powerlessness in the church, and the Father is handing us the keys to the kingdom, saying, "Okay, mighty ones, it's your time to step up with the authority I have given you through the blood of the Lamb!"

## PIONEERS, LET'S SET THE STAGE

Then I heard the Lord say, "This year sets the stage. What you write and legislate from the heavens will become the cornerstone for the days to come."

We have the responsibility to set in motion the things God has on His heart, but with that comes the reality that if we don't, then something else will fill that vacuum.

Will we author heaven to earth this year? Or will we allow man's ways and methods, or worse, the enemy, to fill that void?

I believe that this "setting the stage" means that we have been called to lay a foundation, lay the groundwork, or establish a precedent.

What comes into my spirit is the call to break new ground and pave a new path or way forward that the body of Christ will walk in.

How do we set the stage? We have to recognize the areas God is asking us to prepare for the new in. We have to sow into tomorrow by planting seeds now.

The crops of the last season have ripened and are beginning to droop, and it's time to break new ground and plant what we want to see become a harvest in the days ahead.

This year is the deciding year of determining what doors we open and walk in and what doors and areas need to be shut. It's a stocktake year of removing the unnecessary extra baggage from the church and casting it over the side of the ship.

We must shift our perspective and position. We have been so focused on the fruit and trying to hoard more fruit that we have forgotten to plant the seeds that others will feed off of in the days to come.

## A GREATER TENSION BEGINS

As the Lord continued to speak, I sensed a greater tension coming upon the pioneers. It's the tension of the call to DEEPER while feeling the call to launch out FARTHER.

It's the call to the secret place and the clarion call of the hour to live at His feet more than seeking the public place, but at the same time, not sitting still or being inactive.

We have already been in a season of extreme delay and pullback, where the enemy has warred against us producing. Those days are over.

This will be a season of deeper wells and greater outpouring AT THE SAME TIME!

Many pioneers have mistaken this tension as inner conflict, but you need to know that this is simply the pull of the new chapter and the reality of what you are seeing and experiencing in the now.

This tension will make you feel uncomfortable at times, but it is harpooning you to the future you are the representative for.

That's right, God is planting you in the future, and you will learn to navigate that line between what is coming and what you see.

This tension will cause you to feel deeply dissatisfied and unable to settle in the wilderness, and it will uproot all places of potential apathy in your life, but the good news is that YOU WILL SEE the goodness of God and the breakthrough you have been praying for.

## THE SHELVES MUST BE SEIZED

I heard Him say, "The shelves of heaven must be seized!" and I knew this was referring to the books, the songs, the blueprints of movements, ideas, strategies, and themes on God's heart that have not yet been discovered.

But the word *seized* struck me, which means: "To grasp suddenly and forcibly; take or grab. To take by force; capture or conquer. To take quick and forcible possession of; confiscate."

This is not just a retrieval or a pickup of goods but a TAKE BACK of what has been both blocked and stolen.

*"From the days of John the Baptist until now, the kingdom of heaven has been subjected to violence, and violent people have been raiding it"* (Matthew 11:12).

Pioneers, your role this year is peeling back the curtain so that the church can see what is theirs for the taking.

It's your role to remove blindfolds and reveal the glorious future that has been shrouded by doom and gloom, and then open the eyes of those who have been stuck.

## THE KEY OF DAVID & THE PSALMIST'S DETOUR

However, the key you possess this year is not just the key of authority and access but the key of David. It's the key of worship and priesthood that has been lost.

I feel this so strongly. There is a new sound of worship rising this year onward that is going to break the church out of the glass ceiling of man's ability and restore the raw cry of a generation that must have Jesus at all costs.

The radio edit can inspire and it can definitely encourage, but the Lord is looking for those who will put the emphasis back on the altar floor over the studio room. He is looking for those who will run into the secret place and not leave until they carry HIS SONGS and HIS MELODIES.

For there has been a subtle spoiling of the ointment in the camp of the Levites, but God is bringing a refining this year to distinguish between the musicians and the worshippers.

And He is calling the worshippers deeper, and there will be personal revival breaking out in worship communities around the world that are seekers of His heart. And they will begin to unveil the songs of their pursuit.

And they will untie and ungird the bondages around nations. There has been a chokehold around the church, but this fresh sound will break it in a moment.

"Yes, I am handing the key of David to the Davids," says the Lord. "But will they take it? Will they detour from the path to grab hold of it?"

Worshiping pioneers, know who labors among you. Find the other Davids and hold out your hands.

For this year, it is the WAR-ship that will steer the rudders of the armada of God in new and unknown waters. You are that rudder. Lead us well.

## NEW TERRITORY IS FOR THE BOLD

The last thing I heard was, "New territory awaits!" I sensed a hesitation in the hearts of so many pioneers stepping into new and unknown areas.

There are mantles of courage coming upon those who are going to pioneer movements this year. This won't be on you, but you will need to launch. You will need to step out.

When you do, you will feel the grace and strength of God all around you to take land and pursue what belongs to you without it taking you out.

I then saw someone sitting down doing the numbers, or the pros and cons, of going in this new direction, and they kept saying, "It doesn't add up!"

And no, it won't add up at first, but will you miss out on your purpose while things don't add up?

Will you forsake your calling for the sake of having things neat and tidy? Things will look messy for a while. They won't make sense. Numbers won't add up at first and people will not understand you.

BUT GOD IS ON THIS! Step into your shoes, pioneers! There is no one that can replace you!

This is a birthing season for the pioneers, but if you don't birth the new, you'll regret it in the years to come.

There will be an unusual call to risk and a faith to accompany it, so create a margin for things you don't have on your daily planner because God will surprise you with assignments and ideas not on your radar.

There is more favor and fruit on the raw and spontaneous than the managed and calculated. If you are looking and longing to see greater anointing and greater presence, you will have to lean into what you cannot control but that which the Holy Spirit is beckoning you into.

You will accomplish more with less and experience more mountaintop moments than any other season of your life; it will just cost you your plans and expectations.

It's a changing of the guard and a changing of the garb era. Roles and uniforms are changing in the spirit. There are new mantles for the taking and a letting go of the expired capacity you once filled.

There are new roles and nameplates to be filled. You can't stay in the same role and seat that you had in the last season. You have sensed this. You know there is more and you need to activate your new office by putting on that new jacket and owning it.

This is a "buy low" era. God will put His favor on certain avenues and expressions, and it's up to us to discern them and change our spiritual stock and focus.

This is our time. The enemy thinks he has the seats of power occupied, but it's take-back time for the church.

## IT'S TIME TO REWRITE HISTORY, TOO

As I am writing down all these thoughts, I am suddenly aware of something so near to God's heart for us in this hour: the rewriting of history.

The rewriting of the stories of those who have been through the darkest night season in the last few years and have felt like their greatest days were over.

The rewriting of the stories of those who were taken out and derailed, assassinated, and shipwrecked.

The rewriting of those who have been through the deepest heartache and don't see a future anymore.

Let me say this clearly: We wield the pen to take back the authorship from the enemy and his demonic plans.

We get to determine the pages going forward and we get to steer the plot and storyline of history.

With that said, it is burning on God's heart to see the past storyline flipped and redeemed. It's time you and I saw the years of devastation and robbery rewritten, and pioneers, you and I hold the pen.

We are in the season of rewriting the destinies of families, relationships, and marriages. That's why things have come to the surface: because God is doing an extreme makeover and a do-over.

*"Your people will rebuild the ancient ruins and will raise up the age-old foundations; you will be called Repairer of Broken Walls, Restorer of Streets with Dwellings" (Isaiah 58:12).*

Pioneers, we will look through the mess and rubble and call forth the new day and new beginnings in the lives of those who have only seen pain.

We will see hope where, in the natural, there is none, and we will write the songs and stories that tether us to that hope.

We will pioneer the reality of what God is saying, where the media is only spewing lies, and we will make it a reality.

Pioneers, grab your pen and wield it well, and let's go!

*Letter Five*

# BEWARE THE VULTURES

### (A POEM OF WARNING)

*Dear Pioneers,*

Have you seen the vultures circling you, awaiting your demise?

Have you seen them applaud your decision to leave all comforts for the wilderness only so they can soon mock you and celebrate your horrid failure?

They are the ones who could never have pioneered nor ever had the gumption or conviction to do what you have done, so they revel in your misery and make a career out of the rubble of others' ruins.

They are the hunters and looters who surveil you silently from a distance to soon descend to steal and capitalize from your loss.

They are the assassins that smile at your departure as if there is another less hurdle for their own success.

Watch out for the vultures that lie in wait. They act like friends and confidants, but they sell your misery as street gossip for a cheap affirmation.

They are those who made their minds up about you long ago and are only following you to prove their predictions correct.

Pioneers, you need to know. They won't ever stop circling. But if you keep going, you will wear them out and show them for the nasty swindlers they really are.

In your most desperate hour, they will be there—not as help, but as the cleanup crew from a collision.

They aren't interested in your welfare but seem more interested in your donor status.

But as they circle, let it be a reminder that you are not what they are. You are an eagle.

You soar higher and you will outlast them many times over.

For eventually, vultures starve to death on their own lack of ambition, lack of courage, and disobedience.

You can't live your life trying to appease those who stand on the sidelines watching and waiting for you to fall.

Why do you try to fix them? Why do you try to prove yourself to them? You must leave them behind.

You must block them out of your peripheral view and look forward, for in due time, the fruit will show and the risk and the raw faith of your departure into this journey will convert into a beautiful masterpiece of God's destiny upon your life.

And pioneers, remember in this time of vultures circling, the Lord is highlighting to you that you are His eagles and He's giving you discernment in this hour to see through the smoke and mirrors of dysfunctional relational dynamics because you cannot afford in this hour to carry those with you that do not have the desire to fly or to step into the unknown.

If you do, you'll be tethered to them like a bad vow, contract, or agreement. You'll be tethered to that which is dead, stinking, and rotting, and the Lord does not want you tethered to those things anymore.

This is an hour where you will have to make a decision to break those contracts and ties with those people and demonic assignments.

This is the season where not everything is as it seems. A time when it feels like you're playing a game of cat and mouse, where people's motives and agendas all seem murky and muddy, and you're not sure who to trust.

Those that you thought were going to be for you are not, and you feel alone just floating in a sea, unsure of which lifeline is trustworthy and will take you to safety.

DO NOT let them fool you with their twisted and poisonous words. Void of faith but labeled as caution, they will rob you of your strength and vision.

They will tell you it is noble to run into hiding while they have no experience of ever stepping out themselves.

RUN! Do not give in to their demands.

This is the time when you'll only be able to trust the Lord as you lean further into this calling and decision you have made.

This is a time when you'll feel like the sharks are circling you, and you'll have to keep your heart unoffendable from the unexpected and poisonous words that come from those you thought were for you.

This is a time where you'll need eyes to see through the smoke and mirrors of an agenda to be able to make it through to the other side to keep pioneering.

This is a time where you'll have to make a strong decision to depart from the place of rehearsing the misery of your past.

Matthew 24:28 says, "Where the corpse is, the vultures will gather."

In the past seasons of your life, you've rehearsed the death and the burial over and over, and you've gathered misery friends and vultures that have camped in that place, but you cannot live there anymore.

Pioneer, I'll say this again: You cannot stay in the place of death and the rehearsing of your misery season any further.

You've been through the dark night of the soul, but you cannot stay there anymore, for that is where the vultures camp out, and you must depart from that place. You must leave the vultures behind.

It feels unkind and uncaring, but if you stay there, you'll be unable to fulfill the calling of God upon your life. You must depart.

This is a time where you need to have radio silence. What do I mean?

Eagle, you must soar. Look forward. Do not make a scene and do not look back.

This is a time where you'll get calls nonstop trying to gather information.

Give them nothing. Give the vultures nothing to feast upon.

Starve them out, for information keeps their plight alive.

And it is information that gives them room and access to you as you're soaring into new horizons with Jesus.

Don't give them anything. Starve their macabre ambitions.

Refuse to give them a scrap of your process or even hardship, for it is in that which they find their purpose to derail you and to gossip about you. Starve them out.

Watch them grow thin and frail and have to turn to Jesus as they realize they have been operating in a critical and assassin spirit.

Hand them over to the Lord. Stop making excuses for them as they try to strip you of the very thing you're called to do.

It's time to divorce your death season. It's time to lay down that which didn't happen, that which fell short of the mark. It's time to leave your cave, Lazarus.

Take off your bandages.

It's time to step back into health again. For as you decide to step back into health, and the smell of stagnation leaves you, the vultures will no longer have any interest in you. It is only the smell of your imminent death and failure that attracts them to encircle you.

But I prophesy, you are stepping into an hour where they won't be able to encircle you any longer.

You'll no longer hear their squawks or the fluttering of their wings as they wait for you to fall in the desert sun, but you are entering an hour where you'll feel light.

You'll feel the new strength and wind of the Holy Spirit under your wings, leading you into your best days.

*Letter Six*

# BUILD UP THE ROAD!

*"If you live cautiously, your friends will call you wise. You just won't move many mountains."* —Bill Johnson

*Dear Pioneers,*

Recently in the night, I was awoken by a sound like a creaking gate, then I heard, "This path you have been paving will someday be a highway."

This is a message for you, the pioneers that choose at all costs to go where no one has gone before and the builders creating the very infrastructure for future generations.

But first, let me start here...

## SHOES TOO BIG

Pioneers, has your vision come under attack in the last few years to the point where you begin to backpedal on what God showed you in the first place?

Have you slowly made adjustments to the painting, the picture that God first showed you, and now, it's not looking anything like the original artifact?

The Lord in this season is wanting you to go back to His original plan. Even right now, He's confronting disbelief in areas where you have forfeited the true and pure call simply because it looks impossible.

We are not called to move by what is possible and by what is doable in our own strength, pioneers. You must understand that this calling is about partnering with the miraculous.

You must be tethered to that which God could only perform, and you must know you are simply the conduit, the igniter, the pipe that brings that which is impossible to the earth.

If you are only embarking on a mission according to your own ability, your own connections, or what you can orchestrate, you are not pioneering.

You must get back to that which is too big for you to achieve in your own strength.

You must step into shoes that are ten sizes bigger than your feet. Then you'll know you're truly pioneering.

## BUILD WHAT DOESN'T EXIST

And you are called to build that which does not currently exist.

Too many people are simply taking a methodology, a system, or taking that which has already been created and modifying it slightly and calling that pioneering or innovation, but that is not innovation.

God is leading us in this hour to build and create that which has never been seen before.

God is wanting us to see through the lens of innovation and see through the lens of creativity and to be able to construct that which is a missing piece for the church and for the world.

That is where you come in. You are called to fill that void and that gap.

I'm reminded again of the sons of prophets who said to Elisha, "This place is too small for us!" and they knew they needed to build something that would be able to last many years to come.

They were thinking about their current lack in the moment, but they were also thinking about generations ahead.

The interesting thing about this story is when one of them dropped the borrowed ax-head into the water, and they were distraught because that ax-head was not theirs in the first place.

What does this ax-head represent? This ax-head represents the faith to build when you currently don't even have the resources, the materials, or anything to be able to build what God has given you.

It represents the raw faith and simple obedience to do something in front of you before you even have everything you need to do it.

Are you waiting for your ducks to be in a row in this season? Pioneer, are you waiting for everything to be perfect before you step out and embark on this mission to build what God has given you?

Or are you waiting for the money to be in your bank? Are you waiting for the alignments to be "lined up"?

Maybe we all need to take a leaf from the book of the sons of prophets. Maybe we just need to step out today. Maybe you just need to begin to say, "Okay, God, I'm going to begin to cut down the tree, and then see You provide the next."

## BREAKING HARD GROUND

When Christy and I first started doing online courses, we felt silly, yet we knew God had told us to do it.

At the time, there was no one doing online courses, and we had no point of reference, no guide, no map to tell us that we were doing it right.

All we knew is that we needed to begin. We didn't have any special graphics or proper workbooks or systems. In fact, at the time, we were just emailing out Word documents to our students. That's all we knew how to do. That's all we had access to in that season.

We had so many people reach out to us from our past telling us that we were in error, telling us that we were doing something wrong, telling us that we were an illegitimate ministry, telling us that was the stupidest thing they'd ever heard.

But we had to choose to listen to God's voice and build that which did not currently exist.

And we did.

And many years later, a lot of those people either apologized or joined our school.

And that is always how it'll be with pioneering. It'll always feel like that when you pioneer, that many people won't understand and they will not get it. And you'll have to listen to God's voice over the screams and taunts of man telling you that what you're building is illegitimate.

The only thing that is illegitimate is when you choose to ignore the voice of God and build something safe that He did not call you to create.

Are you trying to build something safe right now? Are you trying to stay away from the risky end of the pool?

Are you trying not to offend right now? Are you trying to appease people right now?

These are all questions you need to ask yourself as you pioneer so that you truly stay on track to break the ground God has called you to break.

## PUSH PAST THE OPPOSITION

*"When Sanballat heard that we were rebuilding the wall, he became angry and was greatly incensed. He ridiculed the Jews and*

*in the presence of his associates and the army of Samaria, he said, 'What are those feeble Jews doing? Will they restore their wall? Will they offer sacrifices? Will they finish in a day? Can they bring the stones back to life from those heaps of rubble— burned as they are?'" (Nehemiah 4:1-2).*

In Nehemiah 4, we see a very similar situation, where Nehemiah was trying to build up the devastation of the ruined city, and in that time, he faced untold opposition from Sanballat and his men, who were constantly taunting them and telling them the same thing.

"What are you doing?"

The question I always ask when reading this passage is, why was it such a threat to them (Sanballat and his friends)?

And here it is: It was a threat to them because the success of Nehemiah rebuilding what had been broken down would only expose their own apathy and complacency.

The people that oppose you aren't exactly afraid of what you're building. They're afraid of your faith journey, because it exposes their lack of faith.

Your pioneering journey only reveals or exposes where they have sold out, leveled off, and lost their fire.

Look around you right now. Take a bit of a stocktake with me.

Who is opposing you? Who is subtly cutting you down? What is their motive? Insecurity, fear, and jealousy?

They don't want you to succeed because it will only show them up. Right now, you need to keep your heart right with these people, but you also need to block out their noise.

*"So we continued the work with half the men holding spears, from the first light of dawn till the stars came out. At that time I also said to the people, 'Have every man and his helper stay inside Jerusalem at night, so they can serve us as guards by night*

*and as workers by day.' Neither I nor my brothers nor my men*
*nor the guards with me took off our clothes; each had his weap-*
*on, even when he went for water" (Nehemiah 4:21-23).*

The interesting strategy that God gave Nehemiah in that season was that he told his men to always keep a sword or spear in
hand, even when they went down to drink.

I believe that the strategy that God has for us in this season as
we build is that we need to stay on guard.

We can't be apathetic for one moment. We need to stay alert
and keep building.

Be aware of the enemy's devices, plans, and tactics. Stay sharp,
stay on fire, and complete the task that God has given us.

## RECEIVE THE INNOVATION ANOINTING

Before the Lord gave me the download for this letter, He told me
something very clearly: "I want you to release to the pioneers My
innovation anointing."

You see, I feel like many pioneers in this season have gone to
pioneer without the unction or the specific anointing to operate in
the new.

They've begun to pioneer some new mindsets, new ideas, and
new ways of doing things, but without the ability to create that
which is new and not seen before.

So many have felt barren, empty, or lost because the thing they
need to create or build hasn't quite been downloaded to them.

The anointing to be able to bring that new thing in, the anointing to be able to manifest something unseen into the seen realm—
something new, something unheard of—has not yet landed in
their lap.

It's like waiting for a delivery, but it feels like the green light for
delivery has never come.

If you're feeling like that, then I know that this is for you. God wants you to receive the innovation anointing, the artisan anointing.

The enemy has tried to shut down the creative anointing in this hour preserved for the pioneers.

But today, that which has been held back from you and stopped by the enemy is going to be released to you.

In Exodus, when the Lord had His people build the tabernacle, there were a group of artisans that came together to build it, but two in particular carried a rare and truly God-given anointing to create the tabernacle. These two men were Bezalel and Oholiab.

It's said that God's Spirit empowered Bezalel and Oholiab with talent and intelligence, giving them the ability to work in every kind of crafting, including woodwork, stonework, metalwork, engraving, embroidery, and weaving.

What we see in this story is the innovation anointing. They were not creating something that was just man-made. Do you see that?

They were creating something that was both spiritual and natural.

This is a distinction you need to see today. You are created to create that which is manifested in the natural, but is spiritual.

You're not creating something that is a man-made system, structure, or invention. You're creating something that is birthed out of heaven and carries weight in the spirit.

So right now, I pray for that artisan anointing, the innovation anointing, to come upon you so that you would receive and conceive and birth and deliver the very thing from heaven that God has given you to deliver in Jesus' name.

## IF YOU BUILD IT, THEY WILL COME

Earlier in the year, the Lord had Christy watch the old movie *Field of Dreams*, where a man is told, "If you build it, they will come."

I think as pioneers, sometimes we think of all the "what-ifs." We think of the breakdowns or problems that could happen. We think of all the things that could go wrong. We think of the cost, the work, and imagine in our minds that this is a mission that will most likely end in complete chaos and destruction.

Because it doesn't make sense when you've never seen it before. It doesn't make sense, so how could it work? How could it be a success? Right?

But as we know in this movie, there was something really significant about what he had to build, even though it made no sense to everyone around him.

"If you build it, they'll come."

I feel that in this hour, we just need to start building. We just need to, by faith, get up every single day and be faithful and obedient to what God has given us.

We need to begin to imagine the field full of people worshiping.

We need to imagine those places we are building being full.

We need to begin to imagine that which we are creating, operating in the full extent and measure of what God called it to be.

My question again to you today is, will you build it? Will you be faithful to get up every day and do what God has put inside of you, pushing insecurities and fears to the side?

## WHAT IS IN YOUR HANDS?

When God asked Moses to go before Pharaoh to set His people free, Moses came up with many excuses. "God, I can't speak!" (Because he was a stutterer.)

It was interesting, because God never actually responded to Moses' insecurity in that moment, but He simply said one thing: "Moses, what is in your hands?" And I think the Lord is asking us the same thing today.

You are looking at the bigger picture, and that's great, but are you overlooking the simple?

What is in your hands? What can you begin with today? What can you use and step out into today? Pioneer, what is in your hands?

## YOU ARE THE TIP OF THE SPEAR

Pioneer, you are the tip of the spear.

In this hour on the earth, the Lord is using you to break through the areas, the hard ground, that has been uninhabitable for many generations.

You wonder why God has fashioned and forged you in the way that He has, and it's because He is using you as a sharp instrument, a spear to break through the difficult ground that many other generations have forfeited.

In Micah 2:13, it says, "The One who breaks open the way will go up before them; they will break through the gate and go out. Their King will pass through before them, the Lord at their head."

This breaker anointing that this Scripture is referring to is Jesus, but you have been handed down the same anointing and calling to be the breaker on the head of the church, to lead her into places that she's never been before.

That is your calling and you are the tip of the spear. In this hour where truth is being watered down, you are the tip of the spear.

In this hour in culture, you are the tip of the spear.

In this hour in government, you are the tip of the spear.

In this hour in education, you are the tip of the spear.

In this hour in the marketplace, you are the tip of the spear.

In this hour, in whatever sphere that God has given you, you are the tip of the spear.

And the question yet again comes, will you build it? Will you step out? Will you be the spear that God has called you to be? Or will you be dulled down like many others have been in this hour and forfeit your calling?

I remember hearing this story years ago of Kris Vallotton, who had an encounter with Jesus in the bathtub, and Jesus began to reveal to him all that He would do in his life. And a sobering moment came as Jesus walked off, and He said, "Time will tell whether you believe what I just said over you."

And in the same way, pioneer, time will tell whether you believe that God has anointed you in this way. Time will tell whether you choose to step into your calling or whether you choose to retreat from what God has called you to.

## LEGACY BUILDING

As I'm writing this, I am seeing a vision of a city with an overlay of infrastructure over it. A city where the infrastructure was laid before the city was even built. A city where the planning superseded the growth.

And that is exactly the eyes that you need to have as you build. Are you building for generations to come or are you building just for this moment?

The city that I come from, the Gold Coast, is a perfect example of where infrastructure was laid without vision. As you drive through the Gold Coast, you'll notice that the infrastructure does not match the growth.

The growth has well and truly superseded the infrastructure. We have one main freeway that runs through the whole city, and it is no match for the population boom that has come to the city.

If you go to some other cities in the world like Dallas or Los Angeles, in some ways the infrastructure is a little bit more matched to the population.

We need to think in that way, and we need to think through the eyes of legacy.

What are we building right now? Are we dreaming big enough or are we only dreaming according to what we can do and what we can build with our limitations?

We must think through the eyes of legacy, because, pioneers, you are not called to build simply what you can do in this lifetime, but you are called to build that which will be the floor for the next generation to inherit.

## HEAVEN'S APPLAUSE

As I end this letter, I'm reminded of a dream that I had many years ago, and in the dream I was surrounded by the great cloud of witnesses, and I was handed a baton.

I looked down at the baton and I instantly knew the cost that was going to be involved in having to run with this baton.

I took a big gulp, because I knew that it would mean my life would be changed completely.

It was like that dream marked a demarcation point in my life where I knew I had to make a choice between that which was safe and that which would actually accomplish so much for the kingdom.

I looked down at the baton in the dream and then I looked over at the great cloud of witnesses who were just cheering me on and speaking and praying, and then I grabbed the baton and took off.

And in that moment, it's like my heart let go of everything else that was sitting in there as an idol in my life, and I knew I needed to dedicate my life to running with this one baton.

So as we end this letter, I want to say to you, well done. Well done for choosing the baton, for choosing what is momentarily unpopular and choosing to run with what God has given you.

But know today that God is so proud of you, the great cloud of witnesses are cheering you on and praying on your behalf, and you will reach the finish line. You will finish well in Jesus' name.

# COUNTERFEITS & ISHMAELS

*Dear Pioneers,*

Recently I posted an advertisement in an app in Australia to sell our car. This app is known for attracting bogus offers, scams, and people who just are stingy and not wanting to pay anywhere near the value of the item that you're selling. However, I had few options being here in the US, so I posted it up on this site regardless. Within hours, I received over ten bogus offers, offering not even a quarter of the value of the car, but fortunately, hiding amongst those offers was one serious buyer who knew the value of the car and was willing to pay the price for it.

I was thinking about this and my spirit began to stir. This spoke to me so much of the pioneering journey. Symbolically, when you dream of a car or a vehicle, it represents your ministry, your mission, and the mandate that you are called to. So I knew this car was in some ways prophetic and represented our Australian pioneering season.

Interestingly, when you step out for the Lord as a pioneer, it is not uncommon to receive multiple scams and bogus offers to try to sell you out early in the game.

## TIRING TEMPTATIONS

Think of Esau, who sold his birthright for a bowl of soup and moldy bread. The enemy tries to bargain with you and tries to buy what has cost you so much to steward, and in a moment, he'll take that from you and send you back to the old stagnant place that you've come from.

Here is one of the places to be aware of. He puts the offer in front of you when you're tired, just as it happened for Esau. When you are desperate like that, you are less focused on the price and more interested in the quick fix or the lifeline.

Have you had this happen?

I feel especially right now that this is something on the Lord's heart. I've been feeling that He wants us to be wary of the enemy's sales and marketing tactics that get us off track.

## THE COUNTERFEIT MANUAL

I want to share a story with you that I've never shared before. When we began officially pioneering for the Lord, it was very unpopular to those around us, as I have shared in previous letters.

The Lord had us leave a church that we'd been part of for three years and had built from the ground up with them.

We had no offense in our heart or bitterness, and we had no issues with the church. We were just simply following the Lord where He was leading us and being obedient to Him.

However, they didn't quite see it that way, and for up to a year, we received bullying messages, emails, and phone calls trying to convince us that we were backslidden and in rebellion.

I felt the temptation to go back...to give up and just wave my white flag. There were constant opportunities to go back to where we had come and to sell out, but we knew that we couldn't do that.

But there was no greater test than one that would come one early morning when I received a message from our previous pastor and a pastor from another season. They had joined forces and saw it was their responsibility and right to fix Christy and me and correct us where we were clearly in rebellion and skewed in our vision.

Their message simply read, "We see that you've made some poor choices, and we want to meet with you to discuss your life and your future and help you."

I knew right away that this was an ambush; however, the people pleaser in me instantly wanted to say, "Yes, I'll meet with you." But I knew I needed to ask Christy and she said, "Let's wait on the Lord and see what He says."

That night, I had a very significant dream. In the dream, I was walking into the church we were part of for three years, and I was holding a car manual in my hand. I noticed right away that it wasn't a church, but it was a mechanic workshop, but I perceived right away that they were not fixing cars but modifying them. They were putting new parts on cars, and I could clearly see we were not meant to be there.

As I walked in the building, I was greeted by the pastor with a friendly smile, but then he saw the car manual in my hand and ripped it out violently.

"That is the wrong manual! It is outdated! You must take our updated one!" And he tried to give me his manual, but I refused.

He relented and said, "Okay, let's go outside and talk." He led me out to a park bench, where we sat down, and he began scolding me and telling me that I was rebellious while putting on a loving smile. It was narcissistic, to say the least.

He was jabbing at every part of our vision and every part of our plan, saying that our hearts were critical and harsh.

I was sitting there feeling just completely wiped by his accusations when suddenly this green tree snake appeared and started biting me on the hand.

I snatched it off and threw it into the grass, and it raced back and bit me again, so I said to the pastor, "Let's leave! This snake keeps trying to bite me!" And he said, "He's our church pet snake. He's not here to hurt you. He is friendly."

Then I said, "But he's clearly biting me over and over. Can you get him to stop?" And he said, "You need to let him bite you."

I began to feel poison or venom beginning to affect my body until I began to feel drowsy, and then I woke up.

When I woke up, I knew instantly that I was not to meet with them. I knew that there was going to be an ambush, but above all, I knew that if I'd met with them, it was going to taint and poison the pioneering call in its early phases and potentially snuff it out.

I could feel the protectiveness of the Father, and I knew straight away I needed to decline the offer. So right away that morning, I messaged back and said I appreciated the offer; however, I didn't feel it would be a productive time, and I needed to continue to follow the voice of the Lord.

This was painful for me. Even for many days and weeks, I battled the fear of man. I battled feeling like I was some kind of unbridled wild ox that needed taming and correcting. "Maybe there is something wrong with me?" I asked.

I felt like I was being dishonoring and unloving and I should be open to their correction. I was a little confused.

However, their correction was not from the Lord, but based on something that I could no longer belong to.

I knew that if I'd met with them, it would've poisoned what God had given us and eventually led us back to the very stagnant pool from which we had come.

## A PROTECTIVE MOMENT

I say all of this to say, God is really protective of you right now in this season.

He's protective of what you say yes to. He's protective of who you align with.

He's protective of what you put your hand to right now.

I know you're surrounded by people trying to convince you to settle down, to level out, to not embark on that crazy, risky mission that God's given you.

"Maybe just take it down a few notches," they say.

"Maybe do it when you have the finances. Maybe do it when you have all your ducks in a row, not now. It's too risky."

Really, what they're saying to you is, "We don't understand you. We don't understand your mission."

And by embarking on this mission, it leaves them behind, because they're unwilling to go where you are willing to go.

I guess it comes down to this: What is your price point?

Are you following the Lord in this or are you following people? It's the same question we need to keep asking ourselves over and over.

I feel the Father's heart so strong as I write this. He doesn't want you to let go of what you have already battled so much for. Don't give up!

## PIONEERS, DO NOT SETTLE FOR ISHMAEL!

For weeks now, I keep hearing the Lord say, "Pioneers, do not settle for Ishmael!"

Many are feeling the pressure right now in the spirit, like there's something that is meant to be birthed, but nothing is in sight in the natural.

It's become such a paradox and deep frustration or even grief, because living with that kind of pent up expectation is tiresome.

It's like treading water, knowing land is coming but it hasn't yet come, and that's how many have been feeling: like the breakthrough that needs to come is not coming quick enough.

Many pioneers are beginning to feel restless, hopeless, and despondent.

It's been so long contending and warring, and it's taken a toll to stay in that continual place of believing when it feels like nothing is shifting.

But I feel this warning right now: Do not settle for Ishmael!

Ishmael was the firstborn son of Abraham, conceived out of his own desire to see the promise come to pass in his timing instead of God's.

Right now, we know we're in a season of time where fulfillment must come and we SEE what we have been contending for, but the enemy is on overdrive, playing mind games and trying to lure us into entertaining ways of orchestrating the promise in our own strength and in our own timeline.

This temptation has never been greater than right now. It's the feeling of impulsively acting upon your will and your expectations above waiting for the Lord.

The lie so many pioneers have been hearing is, "Is God even concerned about what I'm facing? Will He even perform it? Will He even do it?"

Let me say this very clearly to you right now: Do not act upon this temptation to make things happen.

We are in a window of time that God is opposing the enemy's plans and roadblocks and shifting major pieces in our lives. It's a time of doors closing and God preparing new infrastructure for the days ahead. It's an hour of the FINALIZATION of the last season's blueprints and OUTCOMES, but they MUST BE DONE BY THE HAND OF THE LORD, not by ours.

As we enter Yom Kippur in September, watch for things to really begin to move and fall into place.

I believe we are entering a jubilee in the church of massive proportions. God is restoring the:

Voice of the church

Influence of the church

Power and authority of the church

Storehouse of the church

Territory of the church

All that has been robbed and stolen in your life is about to begin to shift, because God is re-aligning us to be the head and not the tail, above only and not beneath.

That is why right now you're feeling so restless and longing for the breakthrough more than you ever have.

That is why the enemy is trying to bombard you on all sides with weariness, frustration, and feeling like you just want to give up and settle.

Yes, you could settle. It's so easy right now to go back. It's so easy right now to camp in the place of second best, but is that really the path that God has for you?

Could you really be content in second best when God has been showing you His purposes and His plans for so long? Could you really settle there?

I believe we're entering into the fulfillment era of the church, and even right now as you're reading this, I pray that all the hope deferred and the weariness that has been resting on you begins to shift.

I feel like people right now reading this are in an eleventh-hour in three specific areas. I know there are more, but these are the three specific areas that the Lord spoke to me about and these are the three areas where the enemy is trying to lure us into temptation because these are three areas that God is about to bust and break through in the months ahead.

## POSITIONING

The first is positioning. Many have been feeling the intense desire to be settled and positioned after all these years.

It feels like movement and migration is still upon us, and we are longing to be settled and established.

The enemy has been warring for so long against this with false hopes and false foundations, leading us to places of instability instead of the promise.

Do not settle right now for Ishmael in regard to the location that God has for you. He's repositioning you, but if you hustle right now and get ahead of God, you will set up camp in a place that is not conducive to the calling of God upon your life. Do not settle for Ishmael regarding your positioning. Wait for the Lord. Wait for His timing.

## PROVISION

The second area is provision. For so long, the pioneers have been reliant on manna from heaven to survive.

You've seen ridiculous miracles, faith, favor, and food coming in the mouths of ravens in the wilderness.

You've seen it all, but in the last six months, especially, God has been stirring your heart to believe for the impossible.

He's been stirring your heart to believe for unfathomable provision for the vision that He's given you.

He's exploded your imagination and your mind and had you dreaming of land and being able to build and construct a specific blueprint that He's placed on the inside of you.

But when you look in your bank, and when you look in your pockets, it just doesn't match up.

And there is a temptation right now to just settle, to go backwards, to do what you can manage and what you can do.

Let me make this very clear: Do not settle for Ishmael regarding provision.

Do not go backwards, for I believe in the next few months, we are going to see the beginning of a wave of wealth for the harvest.

If you think the wiping of debts is a huge thing, you wait and see what's coming. For God is not only going to settle debts, He is also about to flood your life with provision so that not only can you be a sower and a lender, but you can build and construct everything that God told you that you would build.

God is right now breaking that poverty mentality off you.

I feel like there's even many who've been holding onto their seed and their bread, and the Lord says to you today, "Release it! Release it today by faith, and watch Me provide and bring in the provision!"

Do something today to break the dam walls and confront that survival mentality the enemy has tried to place upon you in the last few months.

## PURPOSE

The last area I heard was purpose. God has been increasing your spiritual and governmental capacity, and He has placed a new mantle upon you for nations, but there's been a major war on your voice, your message, and your purpose.

There's been a war on your path and launching what God has given you to step into.

The enemy has tried to make you push down the doors that only God can open, or he has wanted you to settle for a role that is far less than the role that God has for you.

Many right now are nervously trying to find some plow to put their hands to, and the Lord says, "Do not touch that plow unless I give it to you. Do not place your hands upon it unless I put it in your hands right now!"

"Do not sign that contract or agreement without Me!"

Even men are seeking you out to put you to work for their devices to build the empires. But the Lord says, "Do not enter into that project or role unless I command you!"

For in this hour, it is so easy to choose something that is conceived by the hands of man and that is manufactured out of your need to feel settled and stable.

"But now watch as I bring it to pass. I want you to step back into rest," says the Lord. "I want you to step back into synergy with My heart and My promises and My purposes and My timing! I want you to rest in Me, and as you rest in My faith, you'll tap into My miracle-working power that will unleash all that is in your heart and all that is in your mind and all that you have desired."

*"Sarah's faith embraced God's miracle power to conceive even though she was barren and was past the age of childbearing, for the authority of her faith rested in the One who made the promise, and she tapped into his faithfulness" (Hebrews 11:11).*

God says, "Pioneers, what is on your heart, I placed there. It is not of your own making. I put it inside you for a reason and I did not lead you on this path just for it to fail now or to return void. No, it shall accomplish all that I desired for it to accomplish. So right now, do not settle for second best. Do not make decisions ahead of Me. Do not jump ahead of My directions. Do not step into alignments that are never ordained for you."

*Letter Eight*

# IT'S ALL ABOUT TERRITORY

*"Enlarge the place of your tent, stretch your tent curtains wide, do not hold back; lengthen your cords, strengthen your stakes."* (Isaiah 54:2)

*Dear Pioneers,*

The war you have been in is all about territory.

Territory is land that belongs to somebody, but many times, it's in the wrong hands and God uses pioneers to take it back.

When God says, "I am giving you territory," it means that He is giving you something that has been under the rule of somebody else. That's why there are principalities, rulers, and those things in different cities and nations.

If you are a prophetic feeler, you know what I'm talking about. You go into a city or a place, and you feel like, "What's going on here?" and you face a battle or a showdown from that principality. There are regions right now that have principalities ruling over them, but we, as children of God, are called to actually take those territories for the kingdom and evict those principalities.

## STRETCH FORTH YOUR TENT PEGS

I believe this is the season that God is giving us territory. God is asking us in this season to take authority and begin to stretch our tent pegs for new territory that He has called us to occupy. I believe that this is a season where God is putting a request to the church: "Take back regions and nations and cities for Me!"

I feel like God is saying, "Ask Me for the nations; cry out, ask and I'll give you the nations. I still want you to speak into individual people's lives, but there is a cry going out right now for the regions and for nations and in your own life right now. Can't you see that I am bringing you from one place of inheritance into another? I'm trying to expand you. I'm trying to show you what I've given you. I don't want you living in that limited place anymore."

## PRIVATE & PUBLIC INCREASE

But it's personal and global. Both of them are connected. You cannot step out and see your own personal territory, your own home and metron of influence increase without God giving you the nations, because they both come in the same package.

God doesn't want to use you globally while your family falls apart. No, that's old wine thinking. He is saying, "I want to change the legacy of your family. You're not going to go through that whole thing anymore; your marriage is not going to be under fire all the time. You won't keep wrestling with those cycles and dysfunctions."

Stretching forth your tent pegs is going to impact every area of your life, not just one or a few, so get ready as you pioneer to see every facet of your life move forward and increase.

## ENLARGING YOUR CAPACITY

In 1 Chronicles 4:10, Jabez prays this incredible prayer. He says, "God, increase my territory," and God did.

I believe that this is the season where God is placing this on the heart of His people and they're saying, "God, enlarge my territory."

In Hebrew, that word literally means "border, boundary, territory." In Greek, it's *Horion*; the word is the same thing, meaning district and territory.

It means that you are acquiring something that is owned and under a jurisdictional rule of someone else or something else.

I feel like God is really stirring up the church and saying, "Are you grieved by that particular thing that is happening in that city that you have inherited? Are you done with feeling limited in health in your life and family? Have you asked Me for it?"

It might be your marriage. It might be your kids, and you're saying, "I'm not happy that we're constantly fighting, God. I'm not happy that my kids are not serving you." And God is saying, "How much do you want it? How much do you want to see Me break through? I'm trying to increase your authority, your awareness of what you already have; your authority so that you step into a place of actually owning what I've given you."

## FAMILY PIONEERING

When Christy and I were married, we had no clue how to have a healthy marriage, but we said, "God, we need to steward the territory we've got."

To be honest with you, it was a long road of figuring that out, but we realized that our assignment and our destiny was connected to that. Because how could we actually take nations and cities and see them become healthy functional places where the kingdom could be poured out if our own home wasn't experiencing that?

That's not to bring condemnation on people that are still walking and pioneering healthy homes, because we are, too; that just means that we're stewarding it.

It's a dualistic thing where we're like, "God, increase the health of our homes, increase our territory, increase the borders of our walls that our legacy is changing in here so that we can believe for it out there, God, and we can actually see it come to pass, because You're the very fruit of the revival happening right now in my children, in my home, in my marriage, in my financial situation. God, You're doing it out there, as well, and we're believing for both." So I believe that God is doing that right now.

## THE STORM & THE INTIMIDATOR

In Mark 5, Jesus and His disciples had just crossed into new territory after battling warfare in the boat getting there. As Jesus stepped ashore, a demon-possessed man confronted Him right away. That spirit was the ruler of the area that they were stepping into, so there was a territorial principality that was meeting them to try to intimidate them.

That's what many people are facing right now. You're facing the pushback from the increase, so what does that tell us? That tells us that you're doing the right thing. It tells us that you're moving in the right direction. It tells us that we're moving in the very space that God wants us to inhabit. So my encouragement for you is, don't take it personally.

All the people that the enemy is trying to enlist to come at you, it isn't about them; it's about the territory you're about to acquire. You do not need to demonize people, you don't need to get into gossip sessions, you don't need to go into all that. It's just sad that they've been enlisted to fight against you in the territory that you are about to acquire. You don't need to worry about them; just keep moving forward.

# TERRITORIAL BULLIES

Now before I move on, I feel compelled to warn you further about the kinds of bullies in regions you will face.

Over the years, living and traveling around Australia and the USA, we have witnessed my fair share of opposition from principalities in the regions we visit.

We have found that the opposition has manifested itself in specific ways according to the type of stronghold of that city, and we have had to grow in discernment to be able to identify them and know how to effectively deal with them.

To be honest, it felt like for so long, we dealt with these onslaughts defensively and didn't seek the Lord for insight prior to these trips, and it beat us up bad. I remember asking a father in the faith how he dealt with these situations, and he said this powerful statement: "I used to get beat up badly, but now I do two things: I fill up before I travel so I'm in overflow, and I step into my office and know my authority!"

But there's another type of opposition in new cities and regions that can be harder to deal with at first. Let me explain:

*"We don't wrestle flesh and blood right? We war against principalities and powers..." (Ephesians 6:12).*

There is a strange phenomenon we have encountered over the years where we have not only faced principalities in regions, but people who have subtly partnered with those principalities! It's messy!

These people who are meant to be stewards and watchmen over their cities become more like watchers and enforcers. Essentially, they are territorial bullies roaming the land, enforcing their agenda, as well as the most pervasive control, manipulation, muzzling, and kindergarten playground tactics.

The most bizarre thing I have noticed is that they tend to mimic the very same characteristics of the principalities of those regions, and instead of opposing and evicting them, become representatives of them.

It can be so subtle you may miss it, but your spirit won't. You can tell something is off, yet it's difficult to navigate, because it's normally very charismatic people in places of authority and influence, and they have created a regime of followers and yes men over a period of time.

So how do you deal with them?

I want to be honest here. I have wrestled with this greatly. I normally hate confrontation and would prefer to have civil conversations, but that's never productive with these people who like to twist your words and lead you into a sudden death conversation of psychological mastery and leave you looking like a critical prophet.

You have to confront the spirit directly.

Again, I want to be honest. I regret not doing this many times. I have tolerated it when I was meant to call it out. I deeply regret moments where I was so bewildered by its clever faux authoritative prowess, I have backed into a corner.

Never compliant, but silenced all the same. And then I watched as these bullies thrived and these cities stayed in bondage.

Why am I sharing this insight? It's time for David-hearted leaders to arise and take down the Goliaths in regions and confront the leaders who have sold out to them.

We have to shift from being insecure and territorial to taking back territories. Playing the enemy's game is getting us nowhere. It's time for the strongmen to leave town and for the church to rise up.

It's going to require skill to honor people while calling out the demonic partnerships and handshakes. It's going to require tenacity to push through when they slander you. But I pray the fear of the Lord and His zeal drives you.

## REMEMBER WHO HAS THE AUTHORITY

So what we can conclude so far as a surety is that opposition comes when you are taking back territory and pioneering for the Lord.

One time, the Lord said to me, "Opposition looks scary, but it's actually scared of you. All that it has is a loud voice and a Johnny Angel magic show, because that guy was cutting himself up with stones and he's got nothing on you. He's just trying to bang some pans and sound loud and scary. It's got nothing; it simply needs to be moved out."

There are so many principalities and powers around the world right now that are being moved out and decommissioned simply because the body of Christ is stepping into that place and saying, "I'm not going to let my city, I'm not going to let my region, I'm not even going to let my street go down in the way that it has been going."

## PIONEERING FAMILY WHILE NOT FORSAKING THE NATIONS

Christy and I have been trying to pioneer ministry family/ministry life with kids and it feels like it's still such a rare model.

We do far less conferences and traveling than others, and we never leave kids behind to travel (they come with us), but after all these years, people still view it as strange.

Because of that, there has developed a real "one or the other" mentality in the church.

I see a lot of people where they have a call of God on their lives, and they don't do anything with it, because they want to pour their all into the home. And that's great, that they're raising up their kids. I don't want to minimize that.

And then there's this whole other way where people forsake their kids for the sake of going out and doing, which raises ministry orphans.

I feel like the Lord is saying that we can do both, that this call is one and the same. We just have to lean into the Holy Spirit so that He can show you how it's meant to be done.

Many years ago, we decided that we were going to do both, and I'll be the first to admit that it's messy and it's not always quite straightforward.

The cry in our hearts has been, "God, this is the place, and we want to see revival first, so we are pioneering it first!" and then out of that space, ministry and other kingdom stuff just expands, and it grows because it comes out of the overflow of God's heart. We can increase in our territory out there and at home and both can happen at the same time.

## MOVING INTO YOUR POSITION

If you look throughout history, most wars have been fought over the basis of land and territory. And right now, there is contention in the spirit as the enemy sees the children of God moving into positions, as though lining up on the battlefield, to take back territory that has been long held illegally in the grips of unworthy and unlawful hands. When God released His covenant to Abraham in Genesis 12, it is interesting that the covenant of a promised nation first required an act of obedience on Abraham's part.

God said to him, "Leave your native country, your relatives, and your father's family, and go to the land that I will show you" (Genesis 12:1).

A breakdown of the Hebrew words of this verse reveals some interesting insights for us in our own season of occupation.

The two words "country" and "land" are the same Hebrew word. It is the Hebrew word *erets* that has multi-dimensional meanings. On one hand, it can be defined as "common land," and on the other hand, it can be defined as "the earth, the world, the nations." It refers to the whole earth under God's dominion. It can also mean "to be firm."

Dominion is the Hebrew word *radah*, a primitive root that means "to tread down, to crumble off, to prevail, to reign, to rule and to subjugate," which is referring to us taking dominion over the enemy and not people.

Given the Hebrew meanings of the words from this verse, we could summarize that God was essentially saying to Abraham, "Leave all of that which has been common, familiar, and comfortable to you and go to the nations of the earth that you may reign and rule. Tread down over the enemy who has inhabited the earth, crumble him and subjugate his rule. Come near to Me and I will cause you to look and see what I am going to give you, consider and discern it with eyes of faith and wonder...gaze upon it joyfully. I want you to enjoy this and see that I will not only provide for you, but give you visions and all that you require to possess it."

So what does all of this mean for you and me in the here and now?

## LEAVING THE FAMILIAR

God is calling you to leave the land of commonality, and sometimes that means to leave what is comfortable. There is an evident separation between the "old" and the "new" land where He is calling you out from a place of common familiarity and comfort.

This part of pioneering can often be the most unsettling, and it is usually where we are the most vulnerable. Leaving something that has become common to us can be a struggle as we leave the old behind. However, there is a warning here: Do not look back. Don't do as Lot's wife did when she looked back at the burning cities of Sodom and Gomorrah... for her heart was not set on the promised land ahead of her, but the land of commonality behind her.

The Israelites were much the same. Their transition into seizing new territory and leaving the borders of slavery was delayed by 40 years, with many not even setting foot in the land they should have inherited. Why? Because their hearts were set on what was behind them, rather than the blazing fire in front of them. Though their hands were bound in slavery in Egypt, they had grown strangely comfortable with it.

God is calling you and me to subjugate the nations from the enemy's control. We are to crumble his plans, tread down upon his oppression, prevail over him, and then rule and reign. This is a seizing of territory where we will tread down upon the enemy's grasp over the earth and crumble his plans. We are being called to defeat and rule where we allow him NO freedom to reign.

This taking back of territories and seizing lands that are rightfully ours will be seen in every mountain of influence as we subjugate the enemy's control over regions, nations, and the entire earth. This crossing-over transition is one where we will see the great harvest of the earth unfold, all because of our simple obedience to keep walking forward.

## SEEING WITH NEW EYES

There is a key that God gave Abraham in this promise of covenant. His first direction was to leave the land of commonality, and then it was to "see" with *His* eyes. The Father never asks you to leave all that is familiar to you without already having provided the way.

If you have been subjected to the chaos that is surrounding you, I want to prophetically release over you right now that it is time to SEE with NEW eyes, with the eyes of the Spirit, to GAZE upon and BEHOLD with awe and wonder where He is leading you.

It is time to dream again. Dream with Him and consider with certainty that He is leading you into a land of promise, a land of abundance. Look beyond what your circumstances are speaking and look into the territory He is giving you.

I love that one of the definitions for the word *see* or *show* (*ra'ah*) is "spy." I believe the Father is going to release strategies to your heart—whether in visions, dreams, or by simply sitting in His presence—where He will cause you to be like a spy on the wall of the enemy's plans, both those against you and against nations. You will SEE what his plans are and be able to subjugate those plans before they have a chance to move into effect.

This is an hour of upgrading of vision, both prophetically and physically. I believe many will have an increase in dreams and visions as God guides them into the promised dominion of territory. Look upon the dreams of your heart and the dreams of His heart for you with JOYFUL expectation and SEE that He is guiding you into a territory that will affect the nations.

## IT'S TIME FOR AN UPGRADE

In Joshua 24:13, we read about the fulfillment of a promise when the Israelites had finally conquered the land and seized their land of Jerusalem. God said, "I gave you a land you did not labor for, and cities you did not build, though you live in them; you are eating from vineyards and olive groves you did not plant."

I believe God is saying to you today that the provision is on the other side of your obedience; take one step at a time. As you cross over by faith, taking the simple steps in front of you, despite the fears and not having all the answers, you will find provision awaiting you on the other side...for debt-free homes and cars, for jobs, for friends and community, for all that you require. All of this is awaiting you on the other side of obedience and trust, in order that you might fulfill the assignment that God has set aside for you in the land of promise.

If you don't know the next step, ask Him. For this covenantal promise of territory you are given is not just for your life, but for generations to come. For it is time to TAKE BACK what rightfully belongs to the kingdom of heaven.

So hold fast, stand firm, look and SEE that the Lord is GOOD and that He has prepared the way for you. Now SEIZE what belongs to you with your eyes of faith, and you will SEE it manifest in the natural. Stop wondering and wandering...and start looking upon your territory in WONDER. Your glorious King is leading you into your promised land. "I just need your yes. I do not need your networking and your orchestrating and your manufacturing. I just need your surrender now. Watch Me do it," says the Lord.

*Letter Nine*

# GETHSEMANE

*Dear Pioneers,*

This is the letter that started it all.

Gethsemane... I've thought about that painful night Jesus endured before the cross more times than I can count throughout my own life.

Not that I would ever want to compare or take away what Jesus went through, but maybe more so because I see the heart of Jesus in that story in a deeper, more real way than the rest of the gospels.

I loved growing up reading about Jesus healing the sick and casting out demons, but in Gethsemane, *He* was the one in deep pain, knowing what He was about to endure.

"Take the cup from Me!"

I think I have said the same thing to God many nights over as I walked through my own dark nights of the soul.

Dark nights, where it feels like you are stuck in the pain and anguish of midnight and morning just never seems to come.

I've been in seasons of turmoil and isolation with no one to call to help, all the while looking around and seeing other believers seemingly skipping blissfully through life.

I've felt like a leper, not a king. Defeated, not the head. Ever felt like that?

Okay, we just got real.

After years of that, it's hard to break through the lies and see a life beyond the pain of midnight and a thriving life beyond the swirl of the storm.

But why am I writing this? Because I need to address the elephant in the room that the church doesn't address—and possibly also the gators lurking in your basement.

## MY PIONEERS HAVE BEEN IN PAIN

Last year, I laid down our thirteen-year promise and journey of having visas in the US down at the feet of Jesus and let Him have them. I felt like I was laying down a child at His feet. It sounds silly to say, but the grief felt that deep.

I bawled like a baby for an hour as years of painful heart-sickness was also poured at His feet until, somewhere in that moment, it turned into powerful worship and my heart was freed from the trauma of an unanswered prayer and I fully released it to Him.

I gave Him my scars and wounds I didn't even know were attached. I laid them all to rest.

I'm writing this to you because the Lord said to me, "My pioneers have been in pain!"

Is that you? Do you feel like you have been living the pioneer life and masking the pain?

Do you walk into Christian environments, and when asked how you are doing, you just do the "I'm doing great, thanks, praise God!" thing as you sit in your seat, struggling to connect because you have 50 arrows in your back, thorns in your side, and gashes in your feet?

Hmmm, see, this is uncomfortable, yet true.

## SHIPWRECKED, SHELL-SHOCKED, & STUCK

Over the years, I have received many, many emails from pioneers who have faithfully pioneered, only to face their GETHSEMANE and been shipwrecked, never to sail again.

Every single email has broken me to read, because I know that scene all too well.

"We did what God asked and He abandoned us."

"I left everything behind and sold everything for Jesus, and it amounted to nothing."

This has been the fate of many pioneers who have been through Gethsemane and never made it through to the other side of the battle.

One of the bloodiest battles of the last hundred years was the battle of Somme France between 1916-1918, where the British fought the Germans in a very horrific battle for both sides.

A young nurse who attended the wounds of survivors from the trenches revealed their haunting memories of the struggle to fight and stay alive at the front in WWI.

Almost every account detailed the long days in the heat and cold, confined and almost sentenced to the hell of war's misery as they daily lost lives and witnessed the bloodbath that the trenches were known for.

The casualties of this war were far from over even after the surrender, as most of the survivors suffered such traumatic mental issues from what they witnessed that the term "shell-shocked" was invented when treating them.

These men who endured such stressful and traumatic experiences daily for two years were never the same again, and in essence, they were still fighting in the war long after the last shot was fired.

I wanted to give this illustration today because, just like these men in WWI, many of us go through the wars of life, down in the trenches surrounded by the mess, and even long after the battle is done, we carry the trauma and pain of it everywhere we go, affecting every future experience, relationship, and dream.

But we can't keep living like this, and we can't let our darkest seasons keep defining us or lying to us about our future.

Yes, there is a future beyond Gethsemane.

## PIONEERING THROUGH PAIN

There is no other way around it. Pioneering will take you to depths of pain and anguish you never thought possible.

It's far from the romanticized adventure painted by the lukewarm church. It's far from the five-star jungle cruise advertised from the pulpit of recruitment pastors looking for their next religious hirelings.

Pioneering will take you past the laughter and ice cream of the gospel and lead you to the garden of Gethsemane, where you will feel crushed beyond crushed and your very soul broken in tiny fragments.

I'm not making a very good case so far for those wanting to be pioneers for Jesus or are already in the middle of it, but I have to be honest.

I have to share the real account of this lifestyle if I have any chance of helping anyone make it to the other side. And yes, there is another side, which I will share at the end of this letter.

Even as I write this right now, I am on a long haul flight with my family, on a journey we didn't get the choice to make in a sense. In fact, one we didn't want to make, if I'm being honest.

In the last three years, I feel like I have experienced Gethsemane over and over until I felt like I, too, was crying tears of blood.

I know what it's like to be alone in the dark saying, "If it's Your will, take this cup from me!" but then finding you have no other option except to keep walking.

I know what it's like to call your brothers to surround you and cover you in prayer during your dark night of the soul, but then opening your eyes to see them sleeping.

Gethsemane is pure pain, and I can't dance around it or make it into a Hollywood musical.

## WE HAVEN'T COUNTED THE CROSS

I don't think this generation has counted the cost. We have reduced the Christian life down to a highlight reel of victories and "on stage" moments without being real about the in between.

We have led others out of the gate ready to take the world but not equipped for the process and preparation that feels like the death and burial of your appetites, desires, agenda, and personal will.

Gethsemane strips you of it all, leaving you naked and bare before the Lord.

So let me ask you again, have you been there?

## THE ONLY WAY TO RELEASE THE FRAGRANT OIL

Pioneering can have some mountaintop moments. It can feel like a garden of intimacy and adventure in so many ways and seasons, but there is another garden, and this garden is Gethsemane.

The garden where Jesus first bled for us. The garden where His spirit was pressed and crushed in agony as He prepared to go to the cross.

The name *Gethsemane* means oil press. It was from that oil press that His broken spirit was poured out for you and me.

Our lives surrendered to this call in many ways can feel like walking through an oil press.

Pioneering can feel like that sometimes; it's this tension between what you see with your eyes and what you know to be true or ahead of you.

It's the pressing of faith and the assurance that what you are clearing the road for is something significant and monumental.

And it's this kind of faith that releases oil...when we choose to trust Him in the middle of the crushing.

But there has to be a prize or a goal. Without that, what are we pioneering for?

Jesus had a goal. He knew what He was in that garden for. Do you? Or have you forgotten?

> *"...fixing our eyes on Jesus, the pioneer and perfecter of faith. For the joy set before him he endured the cross, scorning its shame, and sat down at the right hand of the throne of God" (Hebrews 12:2).*

But what we often forget in Gethsemane is that our darkest, most pressing, crushing moments aren't wasted; they actually produce costly and fragrant oil that becomes three things:

Oil of worship and sacrifice that ministers to Jesus.

Oil of anointing that equips you for your pioneering mandate. Without it, you won't have authority or unction without that office.

Oil of burning that sets you on fire for Jesus and refines your character.

Over the years, I have dreaded the refinery seasons and the crushing seasons, but I have found that I can always trace my life's greatest breakthroughs and acceleration back to the garden of pressing.

No, there is no shortcut. If you want to last the distance as a pioneer, you cannot go around Gethsemane. You need to go through it.

## BUT DO WE EVER BREAK THROUGH?

There's an old Bill Gaither song that sings:

*"Hold on, my child, joy comes in the morning*
*Weeping only lasts for the night*
*Hold on, my child, joy comes in the morning*
*The darkest hour means dawn is just in sight."*

As I write the end of this letter, it's now nine months after my plane ride encounter where this book was birthed and I wrote the middle section of this letter about pioneering through pain.

This was the first letter God gave me, because I can feel His Father's heart toward the pioneers saying, "I know you have been stuck in the middle part of your journey, but there is light at the end of the tunnel!"

You see, we will never have to endure the cross like Jesus did, but we will have moments where everything looks upside down and like we have hit rock bottom. But it's not the end of the story.

We pass through Gethsemane, get what we need for the road ahead, and KEEP GOING!

So yes, pioneers, there is "another side."

I was put on the spot when being interviewed recently when I was asked, "So is there another side? Do we ever see breakthrough?"

Suddenly, my mind started racing, like I was flicking through the pages of my book, the dark chapters and the victories. I saw a repetitive thing—dark jungles and unknown terrain, dry deserts, and deep waters—then finally and suddenly, breakthrough.

"Yes, there is always breakthrough," I said. "If you keep walking, you will always see breakthrough."

You see, Gethsemane is just a front, a facade, a stage set for something God has set up, and that's a land called PROMISE.

Behind every dark night is an upgrade. But to see it, you need to hold on.

Our timelines are all different, but it's a guarantee. It's who He is. And He doesn't lead us where He can't back up what He promised.

Is this still triggering your heart? Is this touching the hope deferred still lingering in there?

Is it reaching down into your soul and purging out the hidden lies? Stop reading for a moment and let Him minister to you.

He is a good, good Father, and He is not leading you on. You may have seen a higher than fair share of dark night seasons, but Gethsemane is just the shopfront for the wide open spaces and territory He has been speaking to you about for years.

As I was asked that question, I was instantly taken back to when I wrote this middle section of the letter, where my heart was in absolute pain thinking of whether I was leading my family to ruin or to victory. At the time, I wasn't sure.

But only a week later, the facade of Gethsemane left the screen and God began revealing what that season was for.

I have spent months upon months in tears as I have seen what looked like my greatest season of death turn into a season of promise and life more abundantly.

But more than that, I've seen His heart for His pioneers shining through. And I think that's the real reason He had me write this book.

For you, the pioneers of His heart who are always leading others into their breakthrough and the church into her next days, but rarely get your own arms held up.

This is for you. This is me holding up your arms.

Now look to Jesus and don't lose your gaze. It will be worth it soon, my friends. Let's keep going together.

# BABEL

*Dear Pioneers,*

I dreamed recently where I was lost at sea with a storm all around me. I was shouting into the wind for help, but no one could hear me because of the noise. I felt hopeless.

When I woke up, I felt like I had lived this but wasn't sure when, at first. Then it came to me: I had lived this many times over the years, but none more than the years 2011-2016.

After a radical encounter with the angel of reformation in 2009, my language began to change, along with deeper convictions and a whole new understanding and revelation of the kingdom beyond the church walls I had known.

My native tongue changed. My previous language of autopilot Christianese was no longer in me, and instead was a language that would erupt out of me without notice and often shock me, along with everyone else around me.

What had happened?

## THE HOT COAL COMMISSIONING

*"Then one of the seraphim flew to me with a live coal in his hand, which he had taken with tongs from the altar. With it he touched my mouth and said, 'See, this has touched your lips; your guilt is taken away and your sin atoned for.' Then I heard the voice of the Lord saying, 'Whom shall I send? And who will go for us?' And I said, 'Here am I. Send me!'" (Isaiah 6:6-8)*

In Isaiah 6, we see a strange kind of commissioning when angels put hot coals on Isaiah's tongue and it activated his true destiny and his prophetic mandate for his nation.

His tongue changed overnight.

Now, let's just park it here for a moment. Imagine being Isaiah's friends and family witnessing this. Let me elaborate. When this encounter happened, Isaiah said something interesting:

*"'Woe to me!' I cried. 'I am ruined! For I am a man of unclean lips, and I live among a people of unclean lips, and my eyes have seen the King, the Lord Almighty'" (Isaiah 6:5).*

So for this letter, let's just creatively imagine that Isaiah, before this encounter, was indeed a man of unclean lips. Let's say as a drastic narrative that Isaiah used to cuss and say unholy things, and maybe as a less dramatic imagery that he was just a man that didn't use his mouth in a holy way; instead he was a gossip.

In the glory, he was so aware of his fallen state that he said that line. Yet God knew his heart and chose him anyway.

But back to his family. What would they have thought when suddenly his tongue changed? What does that mean?

His message changed.

His focus changed.

His authority increased.

His words were lathered in the glory.

His words carried fire and potency.

That would be a shocking change for him and everyone around him.

## PIONEERS OF A NEW TONGUE

I believe we are on the cusp of a new language being formed in the body of Christ. Not a different gospel or a different Bible (I'm not a heretic, I promise), but a language that takes us back to the original purpose and design of the church before it was cluttered and cliché, stinking of hypocrisy, watered down, and lathered in lip service without any authority. I guess the best way to say this is that our language is getting an OVERHAUL, or being redefined. There will be new themes and words we haven't heard before, but there will also be new and fresh revelation given to the words we already have in our vocabulary.

To be clear, I believe this is going to be more than just a new theme for a New Year's type of thing. This is more than that. This is a reformation of the language of the church that takes us out of stagnancy and puts us back into the creative and prophetically potent verbiage of heaven.

Whenever God does something new, it is always preceded by a new language. Why? Language is creative. Words are creative. They go forth and make, create, and build the unseen world into the seen. It's like poetry and prophecy combined, where dreaming and imagining through the heart of God turns into a tangible reality that wasn't previously there. New language changes the landscape of every place it goes, whether good or bad. It can tear down and destroy, or it can build up, but both are powerful in their own measure.

When God spoke in the beginning, He created. Everything we see and everything we don't see (the heavens) were created by His words, and then He did something amazing: He gave us the role of creating with Him.

*"So the man gave names to all the livestock, the birds in the sky and all the wild animals" (Genesis 2:20).*

Even from the beginning, God has placed within us the ability to create with Him and through Him with our words.

Language shapes the culture around us and determines our values and value for others.

Language shapes destinies and carves generals from lifeless rock.

Language creates movements and spurs revival.

Language stirs up faith and causes the impossible to become possible.

Language is powerful, and right now, we need a fresh intonation and deliberation from heaven to shift the church back on its tracks and a people who would dare to speak this new language until it becomes the norm.

## THE WRESTLING YEARS

I was going through my Facebook memories the other day, where you can see what you wrote on that particular day throughout the years. I found an update from 2013 where I simply said this:

"God is raising up a new breed of voices that know how to couple truth with love. Truth that tears down the mixture and compromise of the church and a love that enables us to lead people where Holy Spirit is leading us."

I looked through the comments and my heart sank, going back to how I felt after writing that post, only to find that people that I loved and even generals I adored only critiqued me, battled me with Scripture, and tried to humiliate me or tear me down. Not to mention, family members that made sarcastic remarks which effectively said, "Remember who you are, don't get too big for your britches!"

Wow...

I instantly went back to those days where I wrestled my new-found language. It was painful to live with. In one way, it was miserable to hold it in and dumb it down, but in another, it was painful to post and live with the warfare of words coming at me.

I think throughout the time period (2013-2015), I deleted more posts than I can count and deleted my Facebook account at least thirty times. The wrestle was real.

Does that sound familiar to you? How many times have you done the same?

## BUBBLE VS. BABEL

I was either wrestling Babel inside me or Babel around me or both. In fact, it became so intense that I began to feel like it was a call I felt like I no longer wanted.

So I laid it all down many times and just served in church to avoid it. I figured that if I got busy serving a bigger vision, God wouldn't require me to keep speaking this tongue that people hated me speaking.

But then the bubbling of it would come when I least expected it. The tongue would find its way out and I would be back at square one.

For me, this bubbling came during worship—and often involuntarily. "What was that?" my pastor would say. "Sorry! It won't happen again!" I would say and resolve to keep a closer eye on myself when I got lost in the presence.

Did you know that the word *nabi*, which is a prophetic expression in the Bible, means "to bubble forth"?

When Saul, who was not a prophet, came into the prophetic camp of Naoth of Ramah, he began prophesying (speaking a new tongue), and people said, "Is Saul counted among the prophets?" (1 Samuel 10:11).

When those who were in the upper room were baptized with

fire, tongues of fire came upon them, and they began prophesying in new languages they didn't previously speak.

What does this tell us? That the tongue of the pioneer is the tongue of the Holy Spirit. It's us stepping into HIS LANGUAGE!

So why is there such a war on it?

Think back to the story of Babel, where man and his wisdom wanted to build a building to reach heaven. It was man's ways and man's methods attempting to connect to God without relationship. So what did God do? He gave them all different tongues which dispersed them into different regions on the earth.

Interestingly, the word *babel* means "divided tongues."

Today, we live in a Babylonian system still trying to find God in their own methods and ways, all speaking their own language and walking in their own wisdom apart from relationship with God. It's a swirl of chaos and noise, and the voice of today's prophets and pioneers has a massive task: to pierce through the noise of Babel with the true bubbling forth of the Spirit.

That's the wrestle you have been in. It's a wrestle because we can't stand the noise and we want to add to it. It's a wrestle because we don't want to add to the confusion and we often doubt what we carry.

Sound familiar?

## LEANING INTO HIS VOICE

So what do we do? How do we become the voices that cut through the noise? How do we pioneer something pure when we are pulled on and influenced left and right to adapt and conform?

We lean into His voice all the more.

We can't pioneer if we have our ear in the world or are consumed with culture. It won't work.

Let me ask you, have you ever been through a season where God asked you to separate yourself from everything that created noise or that created conflicting opinions in you?

What if the warfare was just fed through the double mindedness that came from hearing too many things?

What if social media's nonstop comparison game was cheating you of owning your own voice?

## THE LITMUS TEST

Let's do a little test, shall we?

How many of these do you do?

Go to share something revelatory with a friend, but at the last minute, decide to avoid drama and say nothing.

Go to share a word or revelatory thought online and decide not to.

Post online, but then delete later on.

Edit your thoughts to make them safe and less offensive.

Keep quiet on your dreams and ideas in case someone doesn't understand or judges you for it.

Have you suppressed your "bubble" to not offend "Babel"?

## BE THE VOICE

The main challenge we all face is to be a pure voice that cuts through the noise. We often need to stand alone and sound different for a period of time, but that's what we have to do.

So let me ask you, what message has God given you? Maybe you don't even know how to define it yet. So let me ask you a different question:

What do you say or do that rubs people the wrong way? What is the content or focus?

How would you sum it up?

Maybe that's part of your message.

Recently, an Australian documentary came out about a famous Australian singer called Johnny Farnham who wrote an iconic song called, "You're the Voice." The chorus lyrics are as follows:

"You're the voice, try and understand it
Make a noise and make it clear, oh, woah
We're not gonna sit in silence
We're not gonna live with fear, oh, woah"

I felt this was a timely word for the pioneers and prophets right now. It's time to be the voices we were called to be. The days of silence are over.

## CHASING THE BEAR AWAY

So as I was asking the Lord how to end this chapter, He reminded me of a dream I had years ago.

In the dream, a bear broke into our yard and was chasing us. I kept taking our kids to safe spots, but the bear seemed to keep cornering us, then we would escape again. This kept repeating. When I finally got everyone to a safe place that the bear couldn't get to, Christy said to me, "The bear is just a distraction!" and I woke up.

What is the bear? The bear is FEAR... The bear is every dysfunction rooted in fear that robs us when we are called to be a voice for the Lord.

The enemy's main weapon against us is fear, and if we don't recognize it, we can live our lives running away from it and wasting our energy in survival mode instead of getting to be the voice we were called to be.

So what are some common fear tactics of the enemy that you deal with? Here are a few that come to mind:

Comparison

Feeling invisible and unheard

Fear of messing up

Fear of being wrong/inaccurate

Anxiety and depression

Discouragement

I feel like this is a season that God is wanting to show us how to chase that bear of fear away so we can finally get things done.

We have been playing cat and mouse for far too long, and now it's time to kick out the intruder and step into the phase of our calling we were designed to thrive in: the place of knowing our worth and acceptance and enjoying the mission again! Who is with me?

So let's chase fear away. Let's rebuke fear off our voices. Off our hearts! I pray for you now: All fear, GO in Jesus' name!

*"Say to those with fearful hearts, 'Be strong, do not fear; your God will come, he will come with vengeance; with divine retribution he will come to save you'" (Isaiah 35:4).*

*"Have I not commanded you? Be strong and courageous. Do not be afraid; do not be discouraged, for the LORD your God will be with you wherever you go" (Joshua 1:9).*

*"I sought the LORD, and he answered me; he delivered me from all my fears" (Psalm 34:4).*

Let's leave Babel behind and begin to let forth the mighty bubbling of His Spirit, in Jesus' name!

# FAMILY > EMPIRES

*Dear Pioneers,*

The age of empires is over, and the era of family is here again. Somehow, it got lost since the days of Acts. Somewhere along the way, we traded true fellowship for the mission. The mission is important, but it doesn't replace the power of what is birthed through authentic community.

It's both together.

## THE GREAT SCHISM

But in its wake, a monster has arisen—a schism, a Frankenstein of epic religious proportions. Suddenly, the bricks and mortar are the idol, the building is the great prize, and filling it is the only objective.

Bums on seats. Money in the bucket. That's what God wants. Really? Weren't we the church Jesus died for? Weren't we the bride? Or did that change hands along the way and usher in the age of institutions and mega-corporations? We got fired, and the LLC era arrived. Franchises entered the scene. Brands filled the earth with their marketing angle and sales pitch. And in the void of anything resembling real connection, it thrived. Beggars can't be choosers, right? Open the doors, sign the dotted line, let us tell you what God is saying, and let us use you to build our thing.

It looked good. It felt great to be needed. But then came the day we realized that the bricks were sand and the foundations were a swamp of dysfunction and tragic error.

## WE BUILT THE WRONG THING

We woke up and realized we were like Esau, who traded his birthright for moldy bread and soup. What have we done?

We weren't any more connected to God or people. We were disconnected from God, placing our serving before our relationship and our allegiance to the leaders before our responsibility to almighty God. We lost our fear of the Lord. Our reverence and our spiritual compass were off its center. We were more isolated than when we began. We came for guidance and to belong and were now even further from the shore, except now empty, burned out, and disillusioned.

What happened?

We had built empires when we were designed to build FAMILY.

## COVENANT > COVERING

We wanted covering so badly that we didn't realize that what we were really desiring was covenant.

Covering was meant to be freedom, but it brought bondage and control. It was meant to bring alignment and peace, but it brought demonic soul ties and muzzling. We signed the contract and were suffering from its fine print. We were deceived that we were in union with God, but instead were in bed with the spirit of religion and man's conquest. And we were the casualties of war...again. Yes, again. Around the mountain, we had been again in hopes this time it would be different, but we fell into the same trap.

## TEAR DOWN THE HOUSE

I'm saying this to you because we were designed to build a totally different house altogether. The house we were called to build was FAMILY. It's people, it's the body of Christ, it's HUMANITY!

> *"For we are both God's workers. And you are God's field. You are God's building" (1 Corinthians 3:9).*

So let me ask you, what are you pioneering? What are you building? The old house or the new?

> *"Jesus answered them, 'Destroy this temple, and I will raise it again in three days'" (John 2:19).*

What if I were to say that you were called to tear down the old and rebuild the new? Does that mean we dishonor the old? No, but in building the new, we MUST oppose and expose the schism that produced the white-washed tombs of the Pharisees.

## THE CALL TO BUILD LEGACY

To the pioneers building legacy right now over building empires, few will recognize or see what you are building, because it's an underground mission. It's a call to build low and slow while the rest of the ministry world is building fast and publicly. It's a calling that takes place behind the stage and often doesn't look glamorous. It's the call to build the family over the organization. It's moving away from the hustle and building what is organic and homegrown. It's the call to establish deep roots that extend beyond your lifetime and build a future for future generations.

It's a call to address generational strongholds, cycles, injustices, and the breaking of demonic bloodlines to establish healthy ones. It's the call to set new foundations and prioritize health and wholeness over public image and reputation. It's the call to reverse the messes of the institution that built empires at the cost of leaving orphans in its wake. It's the call to forfeit the plans and goals that produce immediate results for the building and pioneering of what takes many years to show above the surface.

Many are in the tension of this call because they no longer feel the pull of the conference circuit or the appetite for the lifestyle they once valued. It feels in many ways like you are going in reverse or have lost your favor, but this couldn't be further from the truth. The Father has thrown His mantle around your shoulders, and you have begun to burn the old plow and begin this new path. If this is you, then you need to know today that you are not lazy, rebellious, in error, or strange for feeling this call. This is the call of mothers and fathers to establish the FAMILY, set the table, and call in the lonely and lost. It's the call to focus on the health of what you are building over prioritizing its stature.

What is the point of building something big if it's unhealthy or compromised? What good is building sandcastles in the sand? Even if it looks magnificent today, it's going to be washed away tomorrow.

## BREAKING GENERATIONAL CYCLES

God is after your foundations. This is the call to raise up your family well, pioneer even healthier marriages, discover God's design in covenant relationships and the house of Acts community, and raise up a generation that knows how to represent the kingdom well. In a time where the anti-family culture of the world has begun to invade the church, God has called many to the frontlines to RE-

BUILD & RESET the definitions and design of God's house so that we can be a force to be reckoned with.

## THE EXPIRY IS UP

So let me say it again, the days of building empires are over. There is no more juice left in that wineskin. The grace period to keep prioritizing bricks and mortar over sons and daughters is over. The heart of God is brooding over family, and if you are looking for what God's pulse is on right now, that is it. Not a fake family. Not a plastic, inauthentic, religious cliché family, but a real family. We have been so good at building structures and administratively creating perfect organizations, systems, and people management, but we have lost the very heart of the Father. If you are wondering what to build, build a family. Repair the family. Champion the family. FIGHT for the family. That's why the enemy is warring so hard after the family and the values of the kingdom family, because he sees that it is the future.

He sees that it is the key that unlocks harvest and an army of uncompromising burning ones. The tide of culture is warring against the family right now, but we get to be the wave that pushes it back. The days of the enemy tearing down our homes are over. It's been an injustice and one that God is correcting. That's why religion can't be our idol and ministry our mistress. We have to protect the home. We can't be lovers of the boardroom more than the family room. We can't keep sacrificing our children on the altar of "doing kingdom." We can't keep letting Disney raise our kids while we are off doing fire-tunnels. We can't keep letting Netflix and computer games numb our kids to the reality of the spirit. We must build the altar in the home again. We have to lead our families into the presence and into a real encounter. This is a change of gears season where God is anchoring us back to what really matters. That's why you have felt an internal shift of priorities, and your appetite has changed.

That's God showing you where He wants you to move. It's a season of stepping into a different flow, off the hamster wheel and into the slipstream of the spirit. It's a season of less is more, and you will be so surprised by what God produces with your yes to the less.

It's a season of taking back the family mountain for the kingdom and stripping false kings of their titles and evicting them from their thrones. It's a season of finally coming into stability and establishing for families who have been in the long hallway of transition for many years.

He is planting you to make you into a pillar, a shade, and a refuge for so many others. This is the birthplace of revival, and this is what the pioneering was all for.

## IT'S IN THE MESSY

This is the season where we are moving away from the manicured to the messy, from ducks in a row to being utterly reliant on the Spirit. But the fruit will speak for itself. Empires have successfully created clones and obedient servants but have failed to raise friends of God who know His voice.

Family is restoring everything that religion has defiled. We are on a take-back mission, and the lost are coming home. The isolated and those camped out on the fringe, rejected, cast out, and those who don't fit the criteria of the system...they are coming home. The table is being spread, and the prodigals are already beginning to run.

And we have to be ready with a ring and a robe. It's that time. He is getting you ready. Right now, He is severing all unhealthy attachments and ties to you. He is setting the record straight over your home. The generational dysfunctions you grew up in are no longer yours to continue in.

This is a season that God begins a new thing in your home. Kingdom legacy is beginning. He has started a new bloodline that begins with you right now at this moment.

I prophesy: Legacy begins here and now. This is where it changes. Our kids will not grow up tormented, demonized, gender-confused, addicted, or unsure of who they are. They will be sons and daughters of God who know their identity and purpose, pursuers of God's heart, and restorers of those who are broken. Our marriages will no longer be attacked, assassinated, broken down, and destroyed. Our marriages will be holy and set apart. Not like the world's ways but built upon the rock, in JESUS' name!

So keep going! Keep building! Keep forging forward on the unpopular path!

# ARROWS AND MORTAR

*Dear Pioneers,*

This letter is going to be a heart-to-heart for those who have experienced persecution in their pioneering journey. I have little control over the writing of these letters, the form, the style, the content, or even the timing. His words either drop into my spirit, or I don't write it. I'm a pen in the hand of a ready Writer (Psalm 45:1), and I have found that Writer to be more than careful about His words, if not poetic, poised, and very intentional about what He wants you, His pioneers, to know from His heart to yours. So here it goes.

## PIONEERS WITH TARGETS ON THEIR BACKS

Earlier in the week, as I was praying, I kept seeing this vision of people with targets that were painted on their backs, and they were unaware. They had these huge sickle-type instruments in their hands, and they were creating paths and slashing through the scrub and bush of untouched terrain.

And I saw these barriers or fences they were coming up to, and I was like, "Who are these people?" And in my spirit, I instantly discerned these are the pioneers who are paving new paths for the kingdom of God.

The reason the target was on their backs was because they were coming up to significant thresholds in the spirit realm that they didn't understand, and the enemy had painted targets on their backs because he was threatened.

They were coming up to significant cultural and social thresholds. Their pioneering had been so significantly successful, but they had no idea.

I looked at their faces, and they were oblivious to what they'd accomplished in the spirit. They were oblivious to what they'd built that was so significant. And they were oblivious to just how powerful and advancing their work for the kingdom of God had been because they were feeling the pain of the arrows that were flying and hitting their backs constantly.

It was the words of slander, judgment, and misrepresentation of their character. It was taking them out.

It was causing them to stop and not keep plowing ahead. It was causing them to feel like God had abandoned them. They were saying, "God, why would You allow people to do what they're doing toward us? Why would You allow this land to continue? Why would You allow those circumstances to keep swirling around us?"

But God hasn't abandoned you. This is the call that you're anointed for. This is the task that you are anointed for.

## THE IMPASSE

Guaranteed, if you ever come up to a threshold in the spirit in your pioneering journey, you will face resistance.

You'll face the sudden onslaught of territorial spirits trying to prevent you from breaking through into new ground for the sake of the kingdom.

Over the years, I've seen the same pattern happen over and over again, where I'm pioneering semi-peacefully with a little bit of warfare here and there. Suddenly, I come up to a place that feels like some barrier in the spirit that I know I need to push through, and I can sense the victory on the other side.

Everything inside me knows I must become a battering ram and break through to the other side. But then, in a moment, I'm hit on every angle.

Suddenly, things are happening in my family—health, finances, strife, division, fires erupting everywhere around me—and I suddenly feel too weak to push forward.

Many times, discouragement has set in, and I want to sit where I am and not move forward anymore.

And sadly, too many times, I have. Many times, I've even retreated and left it for another day.

Does this sound similar to your journey?

But now, knowing what we know, these moments are critical for us to push forward into, not just for the sake of the kingdom but for the sake of finalizing that pioneering chapter that we'd been through.

Unfortunately, we tend to repeat chapters over and over instead of completing them, finding ourselves going around the same mountain of warfare and facing those same familiar territorial spirits over and over, never feeling any more victorious.

But I'm here to tell you today that those days are over. It is time to push through and break to the other side of our pioneering journey. It is time for us to enter the next chapter to experience new realms of authority and blessing and favor that God has for us.

## SAULS ON EVERY SIDE

It is often those impasses that we need to ignore everyone and everything around us, close our eyes, and worship Him.

We charge forward through worship. We are like David, who was rebellious and undignified and worshiped the ark back to its rightful place. The only person in his sight was the Lord.

It's those times that we need to just ignore the throngs of the masses and the words being thrown at us like hand grenades.

And we need to charge into our destiny with total abandon.

I remember in 2020, at the height of the lockdowns and the social and cultural pressure to stay near our homes, all the churches around us were completely shut down as well as caving into the pressure of government systems and culture. Sean Feucht decided to gather and worship on the Golden Gate Bridge.

We knew that it was something that we needed to do to make a stand for righteousness, and we knew it was something that we needed to do to be like David. But more than anything else, we could feel the impasse in the spirit. We could tell that unless a pioneer burst through the lies of the enemy, the body of Christ was not going to have any example of what it was like to persevere amidst persecution.

I mean, have we even been truly persecuted in the West? This was so small and insignificant compared to what many people have faced in other nations standing up for the gospel. But we knew that this was a needed stand. So we stood with Sean on the Golden Gate Bridge, and we worshiped together and we weren't going to be held back.

And that day, a movement began, but then the spears of Saul came out. I remember I saw it one night in a dream. I saw Sean surrounded by spears. I said, "Lord, what are these spears?" And He said, "This is the spear of Saul."

And I knew it was the father figures that he'd had in his life that were suddenly holding up their spears to him to throw at him in the same way that Saul did with David.

And the Lord told me something very clearly: "I'm now going

to fashion the spears that were sent against him, and I'll use them in Sean's life, and he'll be a spearhead for Me in the nations."

## THE 4:14 CODE

About six months ago, I was on the way to a meeting with Lou Engle and a group of prophetic intercessors and dreamers to pray and strategize about gathering one million women on the mall in 2024 when I kept seeing 4:14.

> *"For if you remain silent at this time, relief and deliverance for the Jews will arise from another place, but you and your father's family will perish. And who knows but that you have come to your royal position for such a time as this?" (Esther 4:14).*

Only a week earlier, I woke up at 4:14 with the Lord speaking to me about the rising Esther Movement and the incoming hijack of the enemy to the movement, too. I could feel the enemy was threatened.

So I knew this event was going to be significant, but for whatever reason, I did not feel a release in my spirit, as I'd not fully understood what the Lord meant or where the attack was going to come from.

But as we arrived and sat around this circle together, a new friend of ours, an amazing prophet from Nigeria, Folaki Kellogg, stood up and shared a dream she'd only had days earlier about Esther 4:14 and how the Lord led her to Nehemiah 4:14 and said that there was going to be significant resistance against the rising of God's people, especially God's orders for this movement.

And He said there was going to be a great persecution from the enemy, but not to be swayed or not to be moved by it.

> *"After I looked things over, I stood up and said to the nobles, the officials, and the rest of the people, 'Don't be afraid of them. Re-*

*member the Lord, who is great and awesome, and fight for your families, your sons and your daughters, your wives, and your homes"* (Nehemiah 4:14).

In this chapter of Nehemiah, you learn about Sanballat and how he did everything he could to stand against Nehemiah as he was rebuilding the fallen walls.

This is what pioneers face. This is the enemy's playbook against the rising of God's people called for such a time as this.

But as I went home that day, I felt like the Lord was leading me to other 4:14 Scriptures and showing me how there were significant pieces of encouragement for the pioneers out there and strategies to keep pioneering. Let me break them down for you.

Pioneers, be quiet amidst the enemy's chatter. Be bold!

*"For if you remain silent at this time, relief and deliverance for the Jews will arise from another place, but you and your father's family will perish. And who knows but that you have come to your royal position for such a time as this?"* (Esther 4:14).

Pioneers, in persecution, you need to go drink more and be filled up more.

*"But whoever drinks the water I give them will never thirst. Indeed, the water I give them will become in them a spring of water welling up to eternal life"* (John 4:14).

Pioneers, you need to stay focused on Jesus and the finished work of the cross.

*"Then we will no longer be infants, tossed back and forth by the waves, and blown here and there by every wind of teaching and by the cunning and craftiness of people in their deceitful scheming"* (Ephesians 4:14).

Pioneers, you need to trust the Lord in this process.

*"Inasmuch then as we [believers] have a great High Priest who has [already ascended and] passed through the heavens, Jesus the Son of God, let us hold fast our confession [of faith and cling tenaciously to our absolute trust in Him as Savior]" (Hebrews 4:14 AMP).*

## IT ONLY PULLS BACK THE BOW

Opposition, when you are building and forging something new, is not only expected, but it's actually part of the process.

Let me say that again. Pioneers, opposition is a part of the process.

God doesn't orchestrate it. He doesn't design it. He doesn't send it, but He will use it for your benefit and for your favor if you allow Him to do so.

For many years, I used to cry to the Lord and say, "Lord, why me? Why have I been through what I've been through at such a young age? But others seem to just be coasting through their Christian life with ease."

And He said to me, "Nate, look around. Look at the blessing and look at the favor that I've given you because of it. Because you've chosen to stay with Me. You've chosen to keep your heart right. Amidst these battles, I've advanced you beyond your years, I've given you favor beyond your years, I've given you wisdom. I've given you influence beyond your years."

If we allow it, opposition in the midst of pioneering will actually advance us into realms of favor that we never could have imagined.

I love the story of Graham Cook, where one late night, as he was about to leave his office, a warlock called him up and began cursing him.

Three months later, after many, many months of his ministry booming and experiencing new levels of favor, that same warlock called him up again to tell him that Jesus had met him and he'd become a Christian. Graham then got to tell him the testimony that ever since that night that the man had called up and cursed him, his ministry tripled in favor, influence, and blessing.

Why? Because every weapon that is forged against you doesn't prosper. In fact, it turns into blessing.

*"'No weapon formed against you shall prosper, and you will refute every tongue that accuses you. This is the heritage of the servants of the LORD, and their vindication is from Me,' declares the LORD" (Isaiah 54:17).*

God uses the things that the enemy sends against you to bless you. It is the pulling back of the bow. It feels like a decrease. It feels like a demotion, but it actually sends us into new realms of favor and blessing that we could not have experienced if that bow had not been pulled back.

And what happens when the bow is pulled back? The arrow is sent farther and farther and is able to hit its mark with more precision and force than it could have without that opposition.

I think it's important for me to use the analogy of a bow because the arrows that the enemy sends at us only become the same weapons we use back. Does that make sense?

They are the same arsenal that we use to advance the kingdom of God. Wow!

Do not be afraid of those arrows, for right now, the Lord is plucking them out of your back, and He's placing them in your quiver for war.

He's removing the trauma, the wounds that have been sustained by them, healing them, and He's putting those same arrows in your hands to be placed in your bow to hit the mark.

## THE SUPERIOR WEAPON

It's interesting to note that in that passage of Isaiah 54, it says,

*"No weapon formed against you will prosper. And every lying tongue that rises up against you in judgment, you shall show to be in the wrong."*

But hear this, it also says:

*"For I have created the destroyer to destroy."*

What does this mean? It means that the enemy's weapons are not only futile, but God has created a better weapon.

In one of the Avengers movies, Thor had his hammer, his iconic hammer, stolen from him, and he needed to create a new weapon. So he finds this person who can create and forge a new hammer for him. The interesting thing is that he forged it from two separate objects, but it became stronger than the first and almost indestructible against any other weapon.

When I watched that, I remember thinking about this verse. God's weapon is so much stronger than anything the enemy could throw at you.

We often feel like Satan has the upper hand on everything in warfare, but God has promised that He has crafted a weapon that is so much more superior than anything the enemy could ever throw at you.

He's protecting you. Don't count yourself out just because you are battered and weary from your pioneering journey. Don't think that this is the end. You just haven't seen that hammer yet. You just haven't seen that weapon that God's forged for you yet, but He's picking it up, and He's wielding it, and He's ready to take out your enemies before you.

## PROMOTION LOOKS LIKE THIS

Over the years, I've noticed a trend. When I'm getting close to a breakthrough and about to step into a new level of authority, anointing, and favor, the enemy sends people in droves to slander me, curse me, troll me, and bombard me on all sides with lies from the pit of hell. It used to shake me, but now it just gets me excited, because I've been here before, and this is what PROMOTION looks like!

Yes, over the years, I've been at this place many, many times before, and I've seen the same patterns emerging in the spirit realm. I've seen the same chaos trying to chase my family. I've seen sickness trying to rear its head, financial decay, discouragement, defeat, weariness, and then a sudden onslaught of slander and character assassination. It's when you are already down, but the boot gets kicked in even deeper. Ouch.

I know this pattern. I know what it's about. It's when the enemy is screaming over and over, "Demotion, demotion, demotion. You have failed!"

But I want to tell you today what it really means. It's the Lord saying over you, "Promotion, promotion, promotion!"

This is the sign that you are entering into a promotion season, not a demotion season.

Let me share one last story with you. In 2022, when we were stuck back in Australia, everything felt like it was falling apart. I remember being in my car one day, and I was yelling out to the Lord, "What am I doing here in Australia? My assignment isn't here! God, I feel like I'm floundering!"

Only two days later, I received an email to my inbox spouting the same words that I'd said to the Lord and using them as a demonic confirmation that I was right.

This man wrote all these curses against us, told us we'd failed, and then said, "Ha ha, you're back in Australia floundering!"

At first, my heart felt crushed, realizing maybe I had failed. Maybe this person was right. Had I disobeyed God? What was going on? And the Lord began to speak to my spirit and said, "No, son, that is not from me. Stand firm and watch what I'm about to do!"

Only three months later, our visas were approved, and we started to plan to come back to America. And here we are.

Yes, I've seen this pattern time and time again. I've seen the word wars. I've seen the enemy's games. I've seen the rising up of witches in my inbox, cursing us, judging us, trying to limit us, hex us. But all of it always falls to the ground.

I've been through the seasons of deep betrayal and the heartbreak of walking through family members forming a resistance against us.

But when you stay at the feet of Jesus, He turns it around, and He turns it all into your blessing.

Let me say that again. When you stay at the feet of Jesus, all of it is disarmed, and He uses it to increase you.

In fact, all of those words fall to the ground like dust, and then God uses them as mortar in between the bricks of the thing that you are building for Him.

Is that not an amazing revelation? That He uses those arrows and turns them into your weaponry or into dust that you use as mortar for what you are building for Him?

Be encouraged, pioneers. This may be a place you have to pass through, but it's not a place that you stay.

*"For every warrior boot used in battle and every garment rolled in blood will be destined for burning, will be fuel for the fire" (Isaiah 9:5).*

## A TABLE PREPARED BEFORE YOUR ENEMIES

No, pioneers, don't be moved or intimidated. This is where the Father anoints you in front of those who can't stand the glory on your life.

This is where He honors you amidst the trials of dishonor, and He exonerates you in front of the Pharisees.

You are His prize and possession. The apple of His eye.

What He blesses can't be cursed. What God sets apart can't be broken apart.

So now it's time to turn your giants into bread!

*"You prepare a table before me in the presence of my enemies. You anoint my head with oil; my cup overflows" (Psalm 23:5).*

## Letter Thirteen

# CLOSURE, EXHAUSTION, & THE NEW PATH

Dear Pioneers,

I want to speak a prophetic word over you.

I recently heard in my spirit, "It's time to dust off your feet!"

You see, many pioneers go through seasons of attack, slander, and mudslinging from the enemy through people, and it can create a negative stigma.

Yes, it can begin to taint the heart of the pioneer and create a subconscious hesitation to step into another season of pioneering.

I mean, I get it. Why would you want to embark on a new journey when you are still traumatized by the last one?

## DREAM OF THE OPEN DOORWAY

I recently had two dreams I want to share with you that are going to paint a picture of what you have been facing (or will face) in your journey.

In the first dream, I saw an open doorway and I was about to step through it when I felt a deep pain or a grief hit my heart, and so I stopped in my tracks. "What is going on?" I asked myself. Then I heard the words, "It's unfinished business." But what is unfinished? Then I began to think of how many personal promises from the last few years have felt UNFINISHED... so many. The grief hit my heart again. I knew I couldn't move on until this was dealt with.

Then I looked down at my feet and I saw mud and dirt on them that I didn't see before. "Wow, that's a lot of dirt!" I thought to myself, very confused that I didn't see it before.

Then right then and there, I knew I needed to remove the mud and dirt. As I did, it was as if I was able to see the witchcraft that had come at me during the last season.

The times I was slimed by people and my name dragged through the mud. The time people flung dirt at me and tried to find dirt on me. In reality, it was never people but the spirit of assassination. Then I heard the words of Jesus saying what He said to His disciples:

> *"If anyone will not welcome you or listen to your words, leave that home or town and shake the dust off your feet" (Matthew 10:14).*

I had been walking with this mud, dirt, and dust for too long and I needed to finally shake it once and for all and move on. So I did. Then I heard a loud instruction: "Forgive them." So I did, and then the dream ended.

## DON'T LET DISTRACTION FOLLOW YOU

As I was processing this dream with the Lord and talking through it, I saw an image flash before me of a magician doing a sleight-of-hand trick. "What was that?" I asked. Then I heard, "Distraction has been the game, but don't let it follow you."

It made sense. It had been years of so much smoke and mirrors and the enemy constantly trying to lure us into fights, situations, and false emergencies and fears that were all show.

Why? So that we would get exhausted by chasing something that didn't exist or need our participation, and take our eyes off what we were really called to.

Distraction was sent to get us focused on who was speaking against us. Who didn't like us. What wasn't working. What could happen, and what didn't happen. All the while, we were being tricked into a sleight-of-hand game. Look back and you'll see this was true. We can't let distraction follow us.

I pray for next-level discernment and wisdom over you right now, in Jesus' name!

## AT THE PIONEERS' CROSSING

In the second dream, I stood at a railway crossing with the red lights flashing, waiting for the train to pass. As I stood, I could see that on the other side of the tracks, my path multiplied into many paths, and so I began trying to look and see where each path led.

It seemed that the path to the far left was pretty straight, and I could see something in the distance in that direction.

Then the path in the middle was pretty much the same—a few more bends, but ultimately it seemed pretty well-trodden and going somewhere.

Then I felt it—the knowing, the pull, or whatever you'd like to call that moment where God changes plans and you have to deal with any previous expectations and adjust your sights on a new horizon. I knew that on the other side, I was called to take the unfamiliar path...yet again.

## EXHAUSTION FROM THE LAST MARATHON

To be honest, my heart sank. I had been on that road far too many times. I knew the loneliness of it and the constant misunderstanding.

I knew there were far more bears to fight there and arrows to deflect. "Can I handle this again?" I thought. Then I looked to my right and left and I saw others like me waiting. "They are probably going to get the easy road. That would be typical."

Then I began to analyze the situation further and ask the Lord, "Is it wrong to long for some reprieve? Is it wrong to desire the road of least resistance for a while? How come others get to enjoy the comfortable road? How come it's not expected of them?"

What was I looking at this new season through? Exhaustion from the last marathon I had just been through. The memories of hardship and the rabbit trails of the last few years.

My heart was starting to feel anger and bitterness bubble up inside, like a kettle beginning to boil. "Peace!" I heard a voice say, and I instantly came to my senses. It was the train master about to let us cross and show us where we were meant to go.

## THE CONFRONTING ULTIMATUM

Out of nowhere, the train screamed past us and shocked me at how fast it was going. The wind from the train's motion pushed us all back and whirled around us as it seemed to go on and on and on.

The train master, preparing to let us cross shortly, simply announced, "Leave everything behind!" "Everything?" I asked in reply. "Yes, you can't afford to be distracted on the other side, or you'll end up lost. So leave it behind." My heart started processing at a hundred miles an hour again, but this time I was self-reflecting. "What am I carrying that I need to leave behind?" I asked myself.

Then I began to hear the judgments and labels I had been carrying from other people. I saw the faces of those who had hurt me, the dark and painful moments I didn't understand, and the hope deferred wrapped around me like a counterfeit mantle. I had seconds left until the train passed, and I knew I needed to make peace with what was behind me, but it felt like a mountain, a roadblock, and a big bag of weight I didn't know how to get through in time.

## THE FACE OF JESUS THROUGH THE ANGUISH

Then I saw it. I saw Him.

Through the tinted glass of the train, I see on the other side a man staring INTO me as if He knew the wrestling match I was in. I stared back awkwardly and kept looking away, then looked back, then away, then eventually locked eyes with Him. I knew who He was, and He wanted me to know it was okay. He wanted me to know I could forgive them—the accusers, the season—and say goodbye to the path behind me. So in those split seconds, I did exactly that.

Whew, what a weight off my shoulders! The train had now passed and we all crossed over, and I stopped at the beginning of this new and unknown path, but somehow I didn't feel what I felt before. I didn't feel like I had been dealt a bad hand. It felt fresh. I felt fresh. I was now ready to move on and embrace the new, whatever that looked like. I didn't need to look behind anymore. I didn't need to prove myself or anyone wrong. And I didn't need to justify my steps. Something was different.

## THIS SEASON, YOU'LL SEE THE FRUIT OF YOUR LAST PIONEERING SEASON

Then to my surprise, I heard a loud noise of people laughing and talking loudly behind me, and I turned to see hundreds of others all joining me on the same path! "Who are you?" I asked. "We have been following you for years, and we finally caught up!" they said.

This is for the pioneers who, right now in this same place, are about to cross over and are feeling the pull of a new unknown or detour.

You have been wrestling a holy discontent and pull to move into a different lane than most yet again.

Maybe you are trying to reconcile your last season and last unknown trek, and the flood of emotions and memories of the trials are screaming at you.

Maybe you are just trying to move out of exhaustion, and the thought of running alone is too painful for you to bear.

Know this:

You are in an OFFLOAD moment. A moment where God is taking care of business and freeing you from every burden you have been carrying.

Something feels different about this new unknown. Get ready to meet the other Wild Pack.

Get ready to see the fruit of your last pioneering season.

Get ready to move into something new. It's time to shed the old and embrace something fresh.

## TWENTY-TWO. CLOSURE, & BRAND NEW DOORS THAT CAN'T BE SHUT!

When I think of doors, I always think of Isaiah 22:22, which says,

"I will place on his shoulder the key to the house of David; what he opens no one can shut, and what he shuts no one can open."

What is this authority being spoken about? The authority to shut doors and open them.

The Hebrew word for *open* in this passage means to "break forth, open wide, and let go free," which speaks to me of the moment of unleashing after being caged up and delayed for so long.

The Hebrew word for *shut* in this passage means to "close up, deliver up, give over, repair, and surrender," which speaks to me of the type of closure God is speaking of, where through surrender and letting go, He delivers us, severs ties, and heals us.

I feel like God wants us to shut doors once and for all. This isn't some Christian cliché with clever imagery. This is the Word of God, your instruction manual right here. It's time you stopped camping out at the door of breakthrough, where you see it but don't hold it. And it's time that you took your keys of authority and closed that door behind you and opened the new.

# LET'S DO BUSINESS WITH GOD

As I was writing this out, I felt strongly that I needed to end this with two invitations to do business with God as we cross over.

First, I want to invite you to surrender your pain and wounds at the foot of the cross just like both dreams spoke of. How do you do this? That's entirely up to you, but if you felt the nudge of the Spirit or felt any pain, anger, and hurt come to the surface as you read this, I want to encourage you to give it to Jesus. Forgive those who hurt you. Surrender your doubts and fears and questions. Give Him your hope deferred and ask Him to deliver you and heal your heart that has felt sick. Lock eyes with Jesus and get your closure.

Second, I want to speak to those who have felt far away from the Lord—just out of sync, out of peace, and feeling lost. Maybe you haven't spoken in a while and don't know where to begin. There are those who have fallen back into addictions and things you feel ashamed of, but don't let that rob you as you step into a new year. Close that door and open the door to life with Jesus again. How do you do this? Just surrender to Him and lay your life down before Him and ask Him to touch you afresh. Someone reading this feels at the very bottom of rock bottom and you don't see a way out, but I want to tell you that your rescue is coming. Jesus sees you and can take away that demonic torment you have been experiencing. The spirit of suicide and death is leaving someone, too. Lord, sever all demonic ties and roots in everyone reading this, in Jesus' name! Shut the door!

Let the new path begin...

# TO THE PIONEERING FAMILIES

*Dear Pioneers,*

Years ago, we received a prophetic word over our family. We were told to stand up in an auditorium as this prophetic minister began to speak over us, not just about my destiny or Christy's destiny, but to the destiny of our children and to our family as a whole.

He began to say, "The Lord has marked your family as a pioneering family, as a prophetic family that would together reveal the heart of the Father into the earth. And the Lord says that you will build greenhouses for others to come into and find family."

And then he began to speak into the individual identities of my children and what they carried: justice, wisdom, creativity. I'd never heard anything like this before except for what God spoke to us about our children.

It was like he was reading a journal and reading the things that God has spoken over our children. For the first time, someone was speaking into and validating the very longing of our hearts to not just be a couple that fulfilled the calling on our lives, but a *family*. He saw our family and what we as a whole would accomplish. It was like a deep settling in my spirit and it forged a deeper conviction to pursue this way of thinking.

You see, for years we had felt different from other ministries and ministers. We had zero desire to travel alone or separate family and ministry, but we saw it as the one and same sacred mission.

What comes to mind when you think of a pioneering prophetic family? Maybe you even doubt that your family are pioneers, let alone prophetic.

Let me just settle that for you. Your family is prophetic, whether you've tapped into that or your children have even begun to notice it, or if your husband has even discovered it. Yet your family is wired to be prophetic. What does that mean? A pioneering prophetic family is a family that simply reveals the heart of the Father through their lifestyle, then God broadcasts it into the earth.

The word "prophesy" in Greek is *propheteuo,* which means "to forthtell and set forth/establish," which means essentially to be the receivers of heaven's frequency and then speak and establish that in the earth. Coupled with the word "family" (*Oikos*), which means "household, bloodline, and lineage," what do you get?

It means a family that speaks forth by divine inspiration what God is doing, and it means a family that forthtells what God is about to do and establishes the kingdom of God through strategies, ideas, and wisdom that God gives them.

It's a family that declares a thing that could only be received from the Lord, divine revelation, and begins to utter the new themes and language of heaven. It's a family that breaks asunder anything that would counteract or disrupt what God's saying or doing.

And it is a family that encourages, comforts, and leads others and the body of Christ into a new day. The word *propheteuo* comes with a command. It comes with an assignment, and that is to create a realm that calls heaven to earth. What does this mean? It means that we as prophetic families have an assignment to bring heaven to earth.

It's a call to pioneer what we see and hear.

We have an assignment to create in our own homes realms of God's presence and glories, miracles, signs, wonders, and revelation so that it becomes a prototype for something that can be duplicated and replicated around the world as your children go out into it.

Prophetic families essentially are gardens, the greenhouses of the spirit where we raise up children and spiritual children that we send as arrows into the world to create realms and worlds out there like what we have cultivated in the garden personally.

So with that said, I want to use this letter today to encourage the pioneering families out there on a few fronts.

## ENCOURAGEMENT FOR THE PIONEER FAMILIES

To those who are pioneering in a healthy way after many broken generations...

It's time to see the fruit of your yes.

It's time to step completely out of all cycles of dysfunction once and for all.

It's time to break generational lines of bondage and establish a new bloodline.

It's time to sever the ties of narcissistic upbringings and all access points the Jezebel spirit has had in your life and family.

It's time to be a family and set the table for others, to become the true family of God that the world so desperately needs.

It's time to pick up your sword and be a voice in this time of history that takes the keys of influence away from culture and gives them back to the church.

Man, the enemy hates pioneering families.

Families that are pursuing God as a unit and march together as one.

Families that have chosen to take the road less traveled and pursue the blueprint of the kingdom together instead of separately.

He loves to isolate and assassinate, cut them off from community, and release the spirit of chaos and confusion.

In his arsenal is deep discouragement that comes like a cloud and tries to settle, hope deferred that he plays on the screens of their minds at night, and torment that triggers past failures and fears.

He knows that if he can keep them in survival mode, eventually they will forfeit the path.

He knows that if he keeps them from their establishing, they will push down the doors of desperation to find it in their own strength.

But today, I hear the Lord saying, "Have I not promised you that I would take you to the land of milk and honey? Did I lead you this way to taunt you and tease you? No, for I am faithful and you will see Me fulfill the promise for you and your family! For just as you have been all in to pursue this legacy, shaking off the bonds of your past and severing old bloodlines, so am I ALL IN to make sure you and your children's children enter into the place I have set aside for them."

This is a season where the enemy is at war against families because they carry something that is revealing counterfeit values and bankrupting his plans around the world.

So we need to leave survival and fighting like victims and go to war.

We must war for our families and our nations with the BLOOD OF THE LAMB!

Today, if you are facing endless warfare against your marriage, your children, and the destiny/legacy of your family, take up your greatest arsenal—the blood of the Lamb—and watch it war for you.

Take communion as a family and surrender your lives afresh.

Cut off all access points and silence the swirling lies in the atmosphere.

And get back to higher ground again.

Pioneering families, you are not lost or too broken. You are not victims.

YOU OVERCOME BY THE BLOOD OF THE LAMB & THE WORD OF YOUR TESTIMONY!

## TO THE PIONEER FAMILIES IN MIGRATION

Dear Pioneers,

You have been peddling, running, and treading water for years, trying to get to the place and season where you will finally settle and catch your breath.

Many are tired and feeling grieved that the road has been so long and the battle to get there has been so drawn out and delayed.

And right now, the joy and passion you started with feel evaporated, but today you need some reminders.

The way forward is NOT stuck.

You are not out of options.

You didn't miss your timing.

You didn't misinterpret God's voice.

You didn't fail or disobey.

You weren't abandoned or passed by.

You just aren't the one holding the map. He holds the map.

You don't hold the timepiece, He does. He knows the exact moment you will settle, and there is a perfection to that timing.

He is faithful. Yes, He is faithful.

What you have experienced in the last seven years is not just warfare against your faith journey, but the assignment of assassination to take you out on all fronts so that you give up and give in.

The enemy has tried to hit your wallet, your peace, your marriage, your relationships, your mental health, and your clarity because he knows that when you settle, you will be a righteous stake in the ground.

He has tried to prevent connection, community, and support by isolating you and bullying you with fears and doubts so that you lose the raw faith that you stepped out with.

What you have faced is the enemy's attempt to prevent you from entering this major promise, because it's more than just you moving to a geographical location. This is about family legacy and revival.

This is the setup for your children and the destiny upon them.

This is the faith move that unties the knots that have been imposed upon your family line and activates purpose beyond what you can see.

Soon the carousel season of moving pieces, families, roles, and assignments will come to a stop and you will find REST.

Soon you will be able to put your bags down and finally feel HOME. Soon you will step into the front door of long-awaited physical homes God has prepared for you.

Soon you will find your people and tribe that you have given up on ever finding in your lifetime.

God is going to make ways AROUND the obstacles you face and loopholes where you will pass through.

He is going to OVERRIDE the negative reports and open the closed gates and ports.

He is going to show you He is faithful and give you signs of His goodness and favor in the weeks to come that He is still the Captain of this earth endeavor. He is still the BREAKER at the head of this migration!

To those who have been shipwrecked by stepping out in faith, is that the end of your story? Did God steal, kill, and destroy, or the enemy? Does he get the last say in your family's journey? Pick up your sword again and get on your face again and commit your future to the Lord, not to man, an institution, or an ideal. Your future is the Lord's, and He who is faithful will deliver.

Get back your warship that MOVES you forward even when the tide seems to move against you.

Get back your fight when it's easier to stay in bed and accept the funeral of a dream.

IT'S NOT OVER. It's just beginning, pioneer families!

*Faith motivated Abraham to obey God's call and leave the familiar to discover the territory he was destined to inherit from God. So he left with only a promise and without even knowing ahead of time where he was going. Abraham stepped out in faith.*

*He lived by faith as an immigrant in his promised land as though it belonged to someone else. He journeyed through the land living in tents with Isaac and Jacob who were persuaded that they were also co-heirs of the same promise. His eyes of faith were set on the city with unshakable foundations, whose architect and builder is God himself.*

*Sarah's faith embraced God's miracle power to conceive even though she was barren and was past the age of childbearing, for the authority of her faith rested in the One who made the promise, and she tapped into his faithfulness. (Hebrews 11:8-11 TPT)*

## A SETTLING IS COMING

Dear migratory pioneers and nomads for the kingdom,

There are held-up outcomes and decisions that will be released in the days to come, and pivotal decision-making revelation and insight will come that is necessary to know how to move and when to move.

There will be the final release of delayed legalities and red tape that will be unlocked, and there will be loopholes and ways to move forward in areas that have looked shut.

The convergence of hardship and promise simultaneously is going to produce not just a new beginning and way forward, but a breakthrough that is going to be like a sonic boom that clears the air and settles the road behind you.

Nomads and wanderers, buckle up just a little longer, because all your transition has not been in vain. But this is the time that for all your moving around and back and forth, God is going to lead you to the land where you will be able to put down roots. Give Him the frustration of not belonging and the pain of feeling not grounded in this process, because you are being led to your nexus.

This is the place where everything you have been stewarding will begin to unfold and be built.

The warfare against you in this convergence moment is designed to cause you to shut down instead of pursuing the final stages of this grand adventure with God. But resist it! Keep moving forward!

This is where migration begins to increase, because God is moving you into position for this phase of your journey.

This is where God opens the way, where it feels like there has been no way forward and no clarity and direction.

Even right now as you are reading this, I pray for maps to open in the spirit and for you to see what you have been too clouded to see. I pray that you will suddenly receive GPS navigation to this place God has been preparing for you.

Pioneers, this is what you were born for. You aren't alone. Keep trekking forward, because your life will be a sign and a wonder of God's goodness to all who see it!

## YOU HAVE MOVED FROM PREPARATION TO POSSESSION & OCCUPATION

In biology, migration is the term used to describe animals, such as birds, that travel from one physical location to another according to the seasons. Human migration, however, refers to the movement of people from one location to another for the purpose of conquest and colonization. But what is the difference between the season you were in and the one you are in now?

In transition, God was focused on removing you from old patterns, methods, ways of doing and thinking, and old assignments and mantles; severing old ties and cycles; healing wounds and trauma; installing new identity; awakening new authority; and preparing you for the promised land and "new thing" you have known was coming.

Migration, however, is the next phase of the process where God spiritually and physically moves you into position to inhabit and occupy what He has promised you. Migration is where you wave goodbye to past limitations and begin to walk in new freedom and authority you haven't known. It's where you begin to walk in your new anointing, new mantle, and new sphere of influence. Migration is where you step into your new role and office and begin to function differently, operate differently, dream differently, and think differently. Migration is where the long-awaited promises begin to piece together and shift in your favor because it's the time of birthing and manifestation after a long season of pushing. This is where you get to POSSESS the promised land, not just talk about it. This is where you get to seize the land, pursue the dream, and occupy the new territory God has given you!

## THERE ARE CITIES & NATIONS WITH YOUR NAME ON THEM

There are so many who are physically migrating right now, whether it's a regional, state, or international move. It has all come in response to your cry for the nations and your governmental call to shift and disciple nations.

Just recently, God showed me a vision of empty seats and imposters in seats of power around the globe. These were seats God was moving His people into to occupy what hadn't been stewarded and to evict the imposters from the seats of power. There are cities and nations with your name on them readying themselves for your arrival to shake it for the King of glory and usher in revival.

## YOUR EXILE IS OVER: YOU HAVE OUTGROWN WHERE YOU ARE

Just as the Israelites stood at the border of the wilderness and Canaan (the promised land) after 40 years of waiting, so now are we all standing at the precipice of a new day...finally. The difficulty is that many have been waiting for so long that it's become kind of the norm, right? Maybe you don't even feel any change at all and can't see any way forward, and that was the challenge the Israelites faced, too. Egypt took a while to break off them. They were born into slavery, but now it was the waiting that had slowly infiltrated their vision and view of the future.

Many have been in their waiting/exile season for so long that when it's finally time to go, it can be daunting. God finally gives you the green light and the next steps to take, and you freeze in fear and strangely grasp for the safety of the waiting season, as limiting as it is.

You have now outgrown the environment you have been in and it's time to move, whatever that looks like for you, because it will no longer be conducive to your destiny to stay there. When we outstay our welcome and plant our feet deeper out of fear, the natural outcome is frustration and bitterness. We begin to blame God for feeling like we missed out while others are thriving, when we are the ones that put on the brakes. The breakthrough you have been wanting to see, the fulfillment you have been wanting to experience, is dependent on you moving onward despite not understanding what you are moving into. Trust Him that it's going to be better than you think!

## LETTING GO OF THE UNFINISHED SEASON

The other difficulty many face when migrating is their grief to let go of the place, people, and old season behind them. Recently, we were praying with friends who are in a physical relocation migration season when I looked at my friend and said the strangest thing. "You need to forgive the land. It was a hard place to be and there was much warfare attached to being there and constant closed doors, but now you have finished well." She then replied, "What is hard is letting go of what we thought was meant to happen here in this season, the unfinished and unfulfilled dreams."

Maybe you can relate. Maybe the place, role, assignment, or mandate you have had has been a very difficult one, and even though you can feel God moving you on, it's been difficult to let go of your own expectations or the feeling of failure you have been carrying. It's time to forgive the season, let go, and move on. Jesus told His disciples to wipe the dust off their feet and move on, and now it's time for you to do the same. As you do, you will suddenly find the fresh joy you need to fully embrace the new season you are in.

## PICKING UP THE NEW CAR

At the beginning of the month, I had a dream where I was standing at a car dealership and I handed in my car and keys to the representative and then waited in the delivery room. After what felt like a while, the representative drove a car right up to me, stepped out, and handed me the keys to my new car.

To be honest, I looked at the car and was a little surprised. It was a convertible car that seemed like it was constructed of many different shapes and models of vehicles, old and new. The representative, seeing my hesitation, said, "Nate, just hop in and check out its advanced features." So I sat in the car and was in awe of the incredibly advanced technology features this car had. I knew right away this car would be able to do more and go farther than the previous car—and possibly even the car I would have chosen.

Migration is not always a physical relocation, but the activation and ignition of a mantle or assignment that is already there, or the upgrade of one vehicle (ministry) to another. Many right now are being upgraded or have already been upgraded, but just didn't expect the car to look like it does. But trust that God's design is far better than your own, and it's now time to turn on the engine and see what the new upgrade can do.

Many ministries and businesses have to reassess their vision and approach in the coming months because we have to adapt to what God is doing. We have to join His slipstream and not just expect we can keep going business as usual. Innovation is needed for us to move with the new wave that is upon us, and we need to ask God for the new strategies and ideas of heaven to help us flow with it.

## THE SLIPSTREAM OF FAITH & ADVENTURE

There is still no map in migration, just raw and blind faith and a hunger to go where His presence leads. As I was asking the Lord about this, He said to me, "I don't give orders. I provide the opportunity to move in faith." This made me think how much of the direction we ask for simply drops within the context of faith jumps and adventure with God. Of course, we want our ducks to be in a row, but He just wants to know if we will begin to move regardless of what we see and what obstacles are around us. What speaks to us louder?

There is a Holy Ghost slipstream in this migration where if we make HIM the main attraction above the destination, WE WILL NOT MISS A THING! So many have been cooped up in exile for so long that they have lost their adventure and wonder, and RIGHT NOW, God is giving it back!

## NEW WINGS FOR A NEW SEASON

As I'm typing out this word, I am sensing that the Holy Ghost is doing a heart work in people reading it. The Lord is saying to those who are struggling to embrace the new season of migration and moving forward that He knows you have been weary for a long time, but He is right now refreshing your body, mind, and soul and giving you new wings to fly. In Isaiah 40:31, it says:

*"But those who hope in the LORD will renew their strength. They will soar on wings like eagles; they will run and not grow weary, they will walk and not be faint."*

When monarch butterflies migrate, they actually grow bigger wings in the process. What looks like it should wear them down only increases their size, and in the same way, God is using this migrating season to increase you and enlarge you. You have only known the weariness but not the soaring, the battling but not the breakthrough. But now God is not only migrating you in the natural, He is also migrating you in the spirit to a higher altitude!

Pray with me: Lord, we give You this season of migration and we ask You to guide and lead us and give us wisdom to know where to go and how to walk out this season well. I let go of what is behind me and fully embrace the adventure ahead of me, in Jesus' name!

*Letter Fifteen*

# THE GIANT KILLER ANOINTING

*Dear Pioneers,*

Years ago, when God began challenging me to step out and pioneer, I remember responding to Him saying, "Can't I just pioneer quietly and stay hidden?"

And there are many pioneers that are in a place of being able to change and affect things while staying hidden. That's true. But God wanted to press a button in me. The button that was avoiding confrontation.

I didn't want the backlash and opposition. I wanted to forge new paths from the safety of my couch, but God wasn't having a bar of it.

I guess if Jesus turned over tables, I needed to accept that I might just offend some people if I pioneered. Oh, and I did. I really did.

What I was about to learn in that season was that pioneers aren't passive, but live on the offensive.

They don't tackle things with a careless attitude, but go into situations with their swords drawn, ready to take ground.

It's what I like to call, "The giant killer anointing."

It's the grit and unction to step up when no one else does and take ground.

It's what Lou Engle calls "being in a pit with a lion on a snowy day," after a book by Mark Batterson.

Standing in front of the Supreme Court a few months ago, Lou told me how that phrase literally played out as thousands of youth stood in a blizzard and prayed for the fall of Roe v. Wade.

He told me how a group of prayer warriors came to DC 18 years ago to pray for the same thing and ended up staying there and starting a house of prayer.

Then it happened. Goliath fell.

What if the pioneering call is bigger than you have been seeing it?

Like David—who knew if he didn't step up, no one else would. It's the pioneering call. The call to break complacency and cowardice off a generation. The call to wield the keys of authority in the earth.

As pioneers, we have the role to step out FIRST and lead the way for the church to then follow.

So Nate, what does that mean? How?

Let me share some revelation from dreams on this and hopefully give you some insight into the anointing you wield to take down giants and lead the church into her days of conquest and dominion in the earth.

I've been stuck on the theme of giant killers for most of this year and unable to move from it, as if there was something God was trying to speak to me about the church and where we're heading.

It's no surprise, though. Look around you right now and you'll see that there are indeed giants before us. Whether you choose to see them as your problem to defeat or not, they are there, and in this next year, God is doing a massive work to engage the church more than ever before to contest the assignments of these giants and serve them an eviction notice going forward.

## PIONEERS AT A CROSSROAD OF COURAGE

One morning in June of 2021, I had a vision of 1 Samuel 17:40, which says:

*"Then he took his staff in his hand, chose five smooth stones from the stream, put them in the pouch of his shepherd's bag, and, with his sling in his hand, approached the Philistine."*

In the vision, I saw myself (representative of the pioneers) picking up the stones, and I could feel the flurry of emotions as David even semi-wrestled this moment between righteous, fiery passion and raw, risky faith. I knew then that God wanted to have a longer conversation with me about the moment we are in and how we are right now, as pioneers and the church, at a place of decision. Will we stand idly by to the shouts of the giants in the land, or will we go and collect our stones?

It reminds me of a dream where I heard the Lord say, "Does My church have to be empty before they will rise? Is it only in crisis and when all is removed that they step up to the frontlines?"

The fact is, we, like the Israelites of that day, are at a crossroads. Our promise is straight ahead and we are surrounded by obstacles and seemingly menacing giants in our path, but the decision we need to make is, "Will we cave in defeat, or will we take our inheritance?" Just like the place where Goliath stood to defy God's people (the valley of Elah), we too are in what looks like a low place, a narrow passage, but a place where we must pass through to further establish the kingdom of God and advance.

## CALLED TO TAKE DOWN GOLIATH'S BROTHERS

In another dream, I was standing with the Lord before a great army of giants, and I was instructed to pick up five stones like David did. Then He looked at me and said very nonchalantly, "Goliath's brothers are going to fall!"

When I woke up, I felt like this was a prophetic mystery waiting to be discovered, like these five brothers of Goliath were somehow linked or were a prophetic snapshot of five demonic strongholds or principalities in the earth we as pioneers were called to take down.

## LORDS OF THE PHILISTINES

Goliath's brothers were called "the lords of the Philistines," meaning they were the elite of their people. The word "Philistine" reveals the root nature of the enemy's plan for these principalities to accomplish. It means:

Destroyers and grievers

Burrowers and weakeners

Dividers and splitters

Multipliers

These "lords" or principalities have been tasked by the enemy to destroy and cause grief, burrow and hide themselves deep in cities and regions, weakening the church, causing mass division, and multiplying. Let's look at the individual giants, too.

## GIANT ONE: GOLIATH

*Goliath* means "exposer, uncovered."

Goliath as a modern principality that would be likened to the assignment of the enemy to keep a victorious church in captivity and bondage. As an exposer, Goliath is an accuser of the brethren and causes much of the mockery of the church we see today in the same way Goliath did to the people of God back in David's day.

Goliath is also what keeps the church in fear and held back from pursuing the inheritance and territory God has given to them.

On another note, the name Goliath represents both the uncovering of the mind and mental warfare, as well as insinuating minds being open or exposed to sinful thoughts and beliefs. Goliath today has still been standing, trying to obstruct the church and keep us bound, but God is raising up a remnant who will say like David, "You are coming to fight against me with a sword, a spear and a javelin. But I'm coming against you in the name of the Lord who rules over all. He is the God of the armies of Israel. He's the one you have dared to fight against. This day the Lord will give me the victory over you. I'll strike you down. I'll cut your head off!" (1 Samuel 17:45-46).

I also believe it's not a mistake who took down each of these giants, and just as these giants represent some of the current giants we face in the earth, so too do the heroes who defeated them reveal a facet of the army that is rising up.

Who defeated Goliath? Well, we know David did. His name has a contrasted meaning of "infirmity, sickness, and weakness" and "beloved." It reminds me of the scripture in 2 Corinthians 12:10, which says, "When I am weak, then I am strong!" And this speaks of the church who feels weak, sick, and disabled being the beloved and approved of God to take down even the greatest and most menacing of enemies.

## GIANT TWO: ISHBEBINOB

The name has a few parts to it, but the main conclusion of the name is that it means to "backslide, settle, retreat, detour from destiny, and be inactive." The second part of the name means to "be from or sits in a high place called Nob." The city of Nob was not a Philistine city but a Benjamite city, so this name could actually be seen as a mockery of God's people and also a counterfeit to our inheritance and occupation of the high places. (As we are the Benjamin generation called to be seated with Christ in heavenly places.)

This principality today can be seen in a myriad of ways, but first, it is the cultural pressure and influence on the church to settle and retreat from the mission and calling to occupy until He comes, which is a forward moving and militant stance. Second, this principality is a counterfeit to the call of sons and daughters to occupy the high places of influence in the earth, and in our absence, it sadly empowers the wrong thing to fill those seats. We can also see this principality in the elitist agenda of power and control of those who have usurped authority and taken the steering wheel from the church.

Interestingly, the hero who defeated this giant was Abishai, whose name means "father of gifts," and we are in a time where the Father is empowering the church to rise up and take His kingdom back from the usurping principalities. We need to know we have authority and access to the "King's domain," the Father's house, and step into our roles again.

The other significant thing to note is that this name also means "many gifts," which speaks of the church. God has handed out many gifts so that those in the church can occupy their unique roles in the many metros of influence in the earth. As we rise up and occupy these spaces again, we will see this elitist giant fall.

## GIANT THREE: SAPH

Goliath's brother Saph has a name of multiple layered meanings such as, "territory border, a marked line or boundary, a threshold, a violent storm or tornado, defending a border, fence-keeper, outside of the borders, breaching the walls, to enter someone's personal space, the bite of a snake, to attack then swiftly hiding."

To me, Saph as a current demonic principality would be the invasive demonic influence in nations and culture. It is violent and nasty and bitter in nature and will cut anything down that opposes it. We see this right now in so many evil narratives and ideologies, and we see this in the media and the censoring on platforms. It's like a storm or a tornado and will destroy and discredit anyone who stands in its path. It occupies a place it actually has no right to occupy and it exerts its dominance and expects compliance.

It's the principality of "me." My ways, my truth, my body, and my experience. It defends the borders of these lies ruthlessly and will attack swiftly, secretly, and stealthily, hiding in plain sight. It inflicts witchcraft wounds by employing the twisted tongues of those caught up in the game.

The mighty hero who defeated Saph was David's warrior Sib-bechai, whose name means simply "weaver," which to me is indicative of the counter-response of the church to be IN the world but not of it. Meaning, we are called to be interwoven into the fabric of society but not in a handshake with evil. It's our role to be the yeast worked into the dough, and the church occupying all places of influence.

Also, from a militant perspective, the word *weaver* speaks to me of the skill of battle and clever strategies to outwit and outsmart the enemy. There is a godly wisdom we possess that carries the presence of heaven in it, that when spoken to these ideologies and narratives, begins to disarm and destroy the fabric of them. We are the giant killers who will pull the loose thread until it's all unraveled in a heap.

## GIANT FOUR: LAHMI

The name Lahmi comes from the verb (*laham*), meaning both "to eat (bread)" or "to wage war." This giant as a modern principality has multiple purposes, but with the same goal in mind: to rob the church.

Bread is sustenance. It's supply. It's your means to accomplish the call of God on your life. The enemy wants to eat your bread, drain your supply, and rob you of your inheritance. He wants to steal our seed so we have no fruit to show for anything!

This giant as a modern-day principality is at war with the effective and thriving church and our produce. It wants barrenness. It wants stillborns. It's after our babies in the womb so that we are robbed of a generation to bring in the endtime harvest. It's after our finances and to own and manipulate the financial systems of the world.

This giant's name also mockingly means "Bethlemite," which is where Jesus was born. It wants to rob the earth of the knowledge of the very seed that would die and become the bread of life to the world!

The hero that defeated this giant was Elhanan, whose name means "God is gracious" and "grace and favor." This name is the promise of God's favor and supply system. It's God's provision and manifestation of promises that will confound the wise and all those who think we are under their system. This giant will fall, in Jesus' name!

## GIANT FIVE: THE ONE WITH SIX FINGERS & TOES

Now, the last giant had a name, but it was not recorded. It simply said:

> "Yet again there was war at Gath, where there was a man of great stature, who had six fingers on each hand and six toes on each foot, twenty-four in number; and he also was born to the giant. So when he defied Israel, Jonathan the son of Shimea, David's brother, killed him" (2 Samuel 21:20-21).

The little that we do know about this giant speaks volumes. Six is the number of man. Man's ways. Man's systems. Man's intellect. But to me, it also speaks of the perversion of God's design. This principality is responsible for every vile and perverted thing on the planet, and this giant must fall!

The hero that defeated this giant was Jonathan, whose name means "God has given" and speaks directly into the humanistic mentality of this principality. "GOD gives. No one else...GOD." The name Jonathan, to me, points back to God. Like a chiropractic adjustment, to see this principality fall, we must be a people who align ourselves with the heart of God and untangle ourselves from the mixture and perversion we see around us.

The main takeaway from this part of the dream is that God is right now preparing us to take down every giant in our path in the days to come. There has been a lie that has been damaging: that darkness is incontestable. But we are called to be the light! Church, you have been born for this house, because you are anointed and appointed to take down the giants of this hour!

## THE HEAVYWEIGHTS PIONEERS, THE WILDCARDS, & THE FULL HOUSE

So pioneers, let me speak into this moment you are now in.

I know you have been intimidated and feeling the tension of courage and wanting to run. You have been through some massive battles and opposition fighting other foes.

But out of the fires of affliction are arising pure-hearted pioneers who God is right now refreshing and readying for what's ahead. They have only seen loss and defeat, but in this next chapter, they will ride the wave of triumph as God turns the page into this new chapter. I kept hearing these two words: heavyweights and wildcards.

Who are the heavyweights? They won't look like heavyweights on the outside, but they have been through the fires of hell and the season of crushing and are now weighty glory carriers for this season.

The heavyweights of religion (a.k.a. Saul's armor) just won't cut it for this battle. We can't fight these giants with our man-made and institutionalized weapons. We can't fight them with our intellect and knowledge, but only with engaging our spirit. These heavy-weights will move offensively using methods that will confront the stale and powerless methods of religion.

Heavyweights are weighty, because they have been laying in the glory in heavenly realms. We have to fight this next season from our position IN CHRIST in heavenly places and quit battling personalities and flesh and blood. We have to come higher.

Heavyweights don't rely on their own abilities but God's, and they don't run from their posts but rest in the power that is inside of them. We have to stop evading and running from the reality of the enemy's plans and the things taking place on the earth. We have a role and we can't hide from it.

And from the painful process of the past few years, a remnant has risen up who are the wildcards of heaven, who are those who have zero filters and zero motivation outside of loving Jesus. When He says go, they go. No questions asked. They are the ones the enemy is most afraid of, because where most see giants, they simply see another opportunity to hurl their stones into a problem.

They are wildcards because God will use them to torment the enemy in the years to come. Just when situations look bleak and hopeless and the enemy begins to laugh, God will flick His wrist and send these wildcards into impossible situations and expose the enemy's hand.

## THE FULL HOUSE, FIVE STONES, & SHIFT OF THE BATTLE

As I end this letter, I want to just paint one last picture. The last word I heard was "full house," which in a game of poker is a superior hand, but even more than that, it spoke to me that the church is moving into its greatest days. We are going to see a full house. This is revival. This is harvest. This is fruit. What also came to me was that this year will be an awakening of the five-fold like we have never seen before. The FULL expression of the house will be seen. The whole bride is beginning to emerge.

God is looking for those who, despite the rapid darkness seeming to spread, will hear the laughter of heaven booming in their spirit. Because they know that regardless of the way the match seems to be going, it isn't a match for God Almighty, who right now is pouring out His fiery Spirit upon a generation fed up with watching the narrative and story go the wrong way and are rising up as bold as lions to see history written according to heaven.

What if when David went down to the stream that day, he wasn't just collecting stones for his battle? What if he was speaking to us now and prophesying? He had five stones. Five is the number of grace. Five is the whole bride in unity. Five is the five-fold church rising.

What if it was him as a pioneer saying, "Church, the giants look huge, but you have got this. It isn't over. Pick up your stones and take the land!" And the cry of my heart for you and me is a resounding, "Yes, we will!"

The shift that is upon you and me right now is that God is turning the defeated and tired into giant killers again. We have become so acquainted with the obstacles, the facts, the newsreel of defeat, and the constant preaching of the size of the giant. But God is using Davids in this hour who won't let this beat them.

So I dare you to go against the torrent of fear, ask God to refresh your hope, and fight again. Go pick up your stones. Goliath wants compliance and a people who will just lay down and accept what the enemy is doing in our nations, families, and communities, but we won't relent!

Pioneers, our best days are ahead!

# THE SPOILS OF WAR

*"When Jehoshaphat and his people came to take their spoil, they found much among them, including goods, garments and valuable things which they took for themselves, more than they could carry. And they were three days taking the spoil because there was so much." (2 Chronicles 2:25)*

*Dear Pioneers,*

I was 14 years old, and my best friend Jason and I wanted to go on a test-of-survival-skills trek across a 1,000-acre property he lived off. This one adventure would be the first of many for years to come. I have no idea how we got our parents to agree to this, but they did. So we grabbed our horses, guns, swags, and food and started our trek to our destination: the other side of the mountain that lay smack bang in the middle of the region.

Within an hour, we reached a part of the property that we had never been to before, and our clever plan soon fell to pieces as we faced a delay we hadn't taken into consideration. This property had not had people on it for a long time, and so there were no roads and no paths. Just dense Australian bush.

Now, just for those who aren't from Australia, the problem wasn't that we would have to travel through the bush, which can be easily done, but it's because of a very annoying unnatural flora that is dense in some areas that was unfortunately introduced to Australia a few hundred years ago. A viny, spiky weed called lantana that grows like a wildfire, covering bushland and making it almost impossible to cross. I ran from a wild bull in the wild once and dived into a bush for safety, only to find it was a lantana bush. It skinned my arms and left its even more annoying slimy spikes on me as a bad reminder of its ways.

Jason and I stood at the endless wall of lantana around us and knew what we had to do: hack through it with the machete. We didn't back down in situations like this. "We push through!" we yelled. All I remember is, it took us two days of the worst scratches and scrapes in the heat of the hot Australian summer and getting to the end of our water supply. But we did it. We cleared a path to the base of the mountain where the terrain was easier. Success!

That story is on my mind lately, because when I think of moments like that, it reminds me that nothing I have done has really ever been easy. Not that I'm ungrateful. I'm glad because all these situations have taught me to fight. And I am a fighter. Pioneers have to be, or we just shrink back and let someone else do it, and how boring is that? Pass me the shovel and let me dig! I have always wanted to be in the middle of the action. Born with a bit in my mouth ready to charge.

And if you're like me, you know how much hard work pioneering is and the price you have to pay. It's rarely talked about in church and you don't see it on social media posts from those you admire. Instead, you see their glorious "I have arrived" moments. I mean, how bad would those days of us hacking through the lantana looked had we had Instagram back then? You would have seen two teenagers yelling at inanimate objects, slashing at grass all day. Not really a viewer's dream. We tend to favor our glory moments over showing the fight. The battle. The dark nights of the soul. They don't get the light of day, right?

I've even pondered on this lately, personally. Should I share my battles? I don't want to portray a false idea around ministry that it's all rosy. Trust me, it's not. I sometimes envy people who aren't in ministry, because they take a lot less hits. But I don't want to make you run from the pioneering call, either.

But the battle is everything. More than you know. Because what I have learned is that every battle has its spoils.

Let me say that again: Every battle has its spoils.

I'm sharing this intentionally at this stage of the book because I feel like we have been through many hard chapters so far. I feel like I've painted a pretty honest and accurate picture of the warfare of pioneering, but I have not yet shared the other side of it, which, in many ways, is the point of this book: to show you that there is another side.

If you haven't seen it yet, you will soon. And the next time you go through a similar season (and you will), you will remember to keep going for the spoils that await.

It reminds me of Jesus in Mark 4 having to go through the wilderness for 40 days, then leaving with the power of the Spirit He would need for the days to come.

So let this be the first letter where I begin to paint you a picture of what is coming for you. And I pray it prophesies deep and throws hope over the places of your heart that have been shrouded in the misery of the hard years behind you.

## GOD DID WHAT?

I still remember my first "spoils" moment. I didn't expect it, to be honest. We had so much opposition when we started stepping out that we just expected that we would have to keep fighting to prove ourselves. But this was when God clearly began showing up in favor on our behalf.

I realize now it was like we had been fighting and battling for so long that it felt so strange when God showed up to the battle for us. And people began to see it.

This first moment came unexpectedly one night when I was doing my daily broadcast on Periscope. I can't even remember what I was talking about, but the thick weighty glory of God fell on the video and I fell to the floor under it. So did people watching. People started getting healed. Laughing. Encountering the Lord. Something shifted. Something around us shifted. But also something in me shifted.

Maybe I had an orphan or performance mindset up until that season, where I thought that it all rested on me. Or maybe I just didn't have faith that God would endorse me or back me up. Either way, that mindset began to shatter as God began regularly moving in powerful ways. Prophecy was off the charts. Words of knowledge. Details of lives. People being set free. I didn't know what to think. If Instagram had been around, I would have definitely shared those highlights.

What was happening? What did I do? Was it me? No, it was the spoils of war. God was faithful to back me up because I had persevered. It was no longer on me, but this was His thing.

He wanted to show me that He was the God who is faithful to those who seek Him. He wanted me to know that because I didn't give up on Him during the years it didn't make sense, He wasn't going to give up on me. In fact, He wanted to show off His glory through me. And He did, and I'm so grateful. Not because I needed people to see it and change their minds. Not because I wanted people to think I was some super special Christian, but because I needed to know that the Father was with me in this.

I'm a fighter and always will be. But I needed to know that I had Him in my corner and that there was a sunrise after midnight.

And I have a feeling you needed to be told that today, as well.

Pioneers, you have been from battle to battle and fight to fight.

You have continued to stand when others have fallen or given up.

You have stayed true when others have caved in to compromise or traded destiny for comfort.

You have left ALL, and given ALL, for the sake of your calling.

You have left the paved cobble-stone roads for the thick briar and thorns.

You have been battered and bruised, and you have paid a higher price than you expected you would.

You have been war-torn and shell-shocked, and now you walk with a limp.

BUT this is not the end of your story.

This is a season when the reaper will be overtaken by the plowman and the planter by the one treading grapes.

This is a season where the Lord will restore the years that the locusts ate.

This is the season that Ziklag[1] will become your greatest breakthrough.

A season so marked by the favor of God that people will not be able to deny the miracle-working power of God and His goodness over your life.

In a moment, it will all shift for you, and you will be reminded again of the laughter you once had and the joy that is your inheritance.

---

1.    Ziklag is a spiritual land we must visit in our walk with God often referred to as a "place of pressing."

And you will have to see to believe the mighty work God is about to do in your life.

Pioneers, I prophesy over you that your spoils are coming, in Jesus' name!

*"In that day I will restore David's fallen shelter—I will repair its broken walls and restore its ruins—and will rebuild it as it used to be, so that they may possess the remnant of Edom and all the nations that bear my name," declares the Lord, who will do these things.*

*"The days are coming," declares the Lord, "when the reaper will be overtaken by the plowman and the planter by the one treading grapes. New wine will drip from the mountains and flow from all the hills, and I will bring my people Israel back from exile.*

*"They will rebuild the ruined cities and live in them. They will plant vineyards and drink their wine; they will make gardens and eat their fruit. I will plant Israel in their own land, never again to be uprooted from the land I have given them," says the Lord your God. (Amos 9:11-15)*

# SURVIVAL MODE MUST END

*Dear Pioneers,*

In the last letter, I spoke about the spoils of war and how God turns seasons of hardship and battle into favor, but I wanted to dive a little deeper and share something that happened to me in that season of unexpected favor and how it relates to the season we are in right now.

When everything began exploding for Christy and me in ministry, we began to see this unusual favor in areas where we'd only had roadblocks and closed doors before.

You'd expect that everything would be perfect sailing at that point, but what it began to reveal in me, at least, was the state of my soul.

Spiritually speaking, we'd entered into a boom, a period of time where the promises of God were coming alive and coming to fruition at a rapid rate.

And even though I had walked through so much forgiveness

and dealt with a lot of things from our past such as betrayals and backlash, what I didn't realize was, that sitting in the very recesses of my soul was a deep pain and woundedness of having walked through such a difficult period of time.

Just imagine a wilderness explorer, who, after maybe many years of being out in the wilderness, had incurred many wounds, many calluses, and many places of hardness of the heart—that was me.

So on one side, I've got a booming, flourishing, new thing that God was doing. We finally burst through the other side of a difficult pioneering journey into a promised land. But my heart was still stuck in Egypt.

Just like the Israelites when they came to Canaan. They were finally there. They were finally at the place of seeing with their very eyes the thing that God had promised them. But because their heart had been through that wilderness and place of difficulty, they were stuck there.

They couldn't see it. Only Joshua and Caleb could see the potential of what lay before them.

So here I was in 2015, at the beginning of a new chapter, but I had to go through a detox. I had to go through a season of the refiner's fire where the Lord was healing my wounds.

He was bandaging me up. He was carefully pouring oil and wine over my wounds.

It was the most beautiful, yet most intense season of our lives, where I watched God, on one hand, give us influence and the ability to speak, a platform to speak into things we didn't have before. And on the other hand, He was tucking me into Himself, and He was lavishing His love and wholeness over me so that I could be fresh and ready for the season that was ahead of me.

I'm sharing this because I believe we, the body of Christ, are at this place again, where seven or eight years ago, God took me through a pioneering detox.

It was so necessary. And if He hadn't taken me through that, I wouldn't have been able to run the way that I've been running these last seven years.

I wouldn't have been able to pour out the way that I've been pouring out.

It is necessary to lean into those places of deliverance and detox when God leads us there so that we're refreshed and ready for what is ahead.

So with that in mind, let me prophesy over you.

"PIONEERS, I AM HEALING YOUR WOUNDS!"

Pioneers, December and January are a strategic time of healing and detoxing.

It's a time when God is doing deep healing and deliverance in those who have been in a three-and-seven-year pioneering and ground-breaking season.

It's been a season where you entered the battlefield, and it's felt like you haven't left, and it's taken its toll on you.

You feel battle-weary and in need of an internal overhaul.

Many have felt like they have hit a wall in their spirit, their mind, and also physically, and now you (unless you are healed and refreshed) won't be able to step into anything in 2024.

## PIONEERING TRAUMA

Last week, as I was praying, the Lord said to me, "My pioneers need to know when it's time to stop and rest."

Then He said, "My pioneers need to know when it's a season to BATTLE and when it's a season to SETTLE."

I began to think of our journey and how it's been a dance between the two, but the last three years have been BATTLE, and pioneers have been severely wounded in the process.

The battle has been fierce, and the casualties have been high.

Many pioneers who started fresh-faced and full of life are now depleted and dealing with the long-term effects of continual hard ground and repeated wounding from the dangerous path.

It's begun to create a trauma mindset in pioneers and pioneer families.

It's begun to affect how you see and respond to life and shut down the faith and ferocity you need that fuels your journey.

But then I heard the Lord say, "Pioneers, I am healing your wounds!"

*"'But I will restore you to health and heal your wounds,' declares the LORD, 'because you are called an outcast, Zion, for whom no one cares'" (Jeremiah 30:17).*

## NOMADS FINDING REST

Right now, many nomadic pioneers are in a place of feeling spiritually and mentally dizzy.

You have been on the risky "pay whatever price" faith journey, and it's led you to many strange and obscure seasons that don't yet make sense.

It's the wild goose chase, where things don't always work or come together, but you know God led you there.

And now, after many years, it feels like you have stepped off the merry-go-round, and your spiritual equilibrium is out.

Your head is spinning, and you don't know how to put your bags down.

All you have ever known is the GO, and now you are in the place of God bringing you into land, and it's hard to do.

After your head stops spinning, what happens is that you begin to see all the things that need attention now that you have stopped.

Your heart needs time to be still. Your soul is crying out for refreshment and rest.

Nomadic pioneers, choose to rest. Don't run into your next

thing just yet, not before you get refreshed.

## THE DARKROOM SEASON

Pioneers, I know you have been in a darkroom season.

It's a season where not only does the enemy rage hard at you, but it's also a season where it feels like the lights are out.

Heaven seems quiet. Dreams are less. And you have no idea where you are going.

It's like you were paving a new path, then someone turned the lights off.

Now, you can't see, and you don't have any insight into where you are going or what God is saying.

This can easily be diagnosed as a failure season, but isn't a darkroom where photographs go to be developed?

What if this darkroom is not a dead end but the beginning of a new chapter? A revealing?

But regardless, the darkroom can often multiply the state of woundedness of the pioneer.

## THE WITCHCRAFT SLIME DETOX

Pioneers, one of the most critical parts of this process is the healing from witchcraft attacks.

The last three years have been a tough road for those breaking new ground because witchcraft has become even more popular.

The religious have slimed you nonstop for being a supposed rebel and heretic.

The Sauls have slimed you for not putting on their armor and wearing their slogan.

The apostolic moguls have kicked you out for now, bowing down to their elitist agenda.

The eunuchs, who do nothing, have dragged your name through the mud because your yes exposes their disobedience.

The Athaliahs have come after you because you are pure-hearted and without guile.

Jezebel has been after you because you can't be bought and don't dance with culture.

The secret saboteurs close to you have created campaigns to discredit you and shut doors.

And well, let's say it: Some family and friends think you have lost your marbles, so they have thrown daggers and doubts at you the whole time.

But...you kept pioneering anyway, mighty warrior! Wow, what a feat!

But, let's be honest, it does take its toll, and right now, you are feeling like a boxer the day after a big fight. You didn't feel it months ago, but today you do, and the Lord is now DESLIMING you and healing your wounds.

He is pouring His oil and wine over you and restoring you to total health.

He is breaking soul ties and strongholds you didn't even know you had and setting you completely free so that you are UNLATCHED, UNHINGED, and UNLEASHED for tomorrow's assignment.

## TURNING BACK THE CLOCK

On the first of December, I had a dream where I was reliving a painful memory I had forgotten from my childhood, and in the dream, God redeemed it and spoke a new life over it.

When I woke, the Lord said, "I have to go back to launch you forward."

And right now, many are feeling the sudden influx of triggers, and past pain and PTSD come up out of nowhere.

"Didn't I deal with that?" many are saying. But this is a deeper clean to create a greater capacity inside you for the days ahead.

There have been some subtly sabotaging mindsets that have

been clinging to you from those memories, and you won't be able to move ahead effectively while still thinking in that way.

## OLD TRIGGERS & CRISIS RESPONSE

"But why am I being triggered the way I am? It feels like everything is erupting inside of me?"

Yes, it's all coming to the surface right now, because God is not only healing you of your wounds but also recalibrating your emotions and mind and retraining you in how you see and respond to things around you.

A battle season will teach you to react in a *not* spirit-led way.

You swing your sword at anything that comes near.

You rush to put out every fire you see.

You have been cursed and betrayed by so many people that you begin to see everyone as the enemy.

Your heart gets burnt so often that you hide it behind many layers of self-protection.

Essentially, you live in a constant state of fight or flight.

The fight-or-flight response refers to the physiological reaction that occurs in the presence of something mentally or physically terrifying.

You have lived in that place long enough, even for decades, and the Lord is healing you from the triggers of the past and the ways they cause you to react now.

It's survival mode at its finest, and that MUST BREAK BEFORE YOU CROSS OVER!

## THE THRESHOLD

Many pioneers have been at this threshold for too long.

It's the place of tension between the new day and the night of the soul.

You have been stuck at 3 a.m., feeling broken and battered and knowing morning is coming but unsure of how to get there.

Many have been like Jacob wrestling the angel, and now day-break has finally come.

But your hip is out.

You are walking with a limp, and while your name is changed and your new day is before you, you need to heal before you can even make a step.

## NOT ALONE IN THE FIRE

To end this word, I want to share an encounter with Jesus last week that I believe the Lord gave me for the pioneers.

I went into a vision of standing in a furnace with Jesus, but it wasn't hot or scary. It felt like the safest place to be. Then I asked Him why I was there.

He looked at me, smiled, and replied to my question. "You and many are in the refiner's fire because you have asked for more than most."

"What have I asked for?" I asked, needing to know specifics.

"All of me and none of the world."

Then I broke down. I could feel the fire hitting my heart and soul. I could feel it breaking down the trauma and weariness of being in the battle for so many years without seeing an end.

I could feel it tearing down constructs I had built in the wilderness of the last three years, where I believed it was on me.

I could feel the fire hitting the fear and anxiety that had started to build up, causing me to hold back instead of stepping into new frontiers.

I could feel the toll of the nomadic years beginning to kindle like a slow burn, but one I didn't realize needed to go.

I could suddenly feel the blows I had taken from principalities, ones I had just ignored at the time.

I could feel the fire burning away some words, at first, and it was a few. Then it streamed in like a dirty river of curses and judgments.

As this happened, I began to say, "My life has been a long battle, and I need rest!" Then something happened that I didn't expect.

Very simply and smothered in so much freedom, He said to me, "What makes you think this life is your own?"

Then He started to laugh again hysterically, and I came out of the encounter.

I feel I had this for many of us who are pioneering and have done so for some time. This is a message on the Lord's heart for us, showing us why we are in this process.

We are in the fire with Jesus.

The good kind.

The freeing kind.

The kind of fire where wounds are healed, hearts are reconnected, and the road gets cleared ahead while you linger there.

*Letter Eighteen*

# ADVICE FOR UNCONVENTIONAL VOICES

*Dear Pioneers,*

Many years ago, when I first felt the fire of God on my life, I was so hungry for Him that it felt like I couldn't have enough or consume enough of God's Word, His presence, and His voice.

But in that season, something strange happened in me, where it was like I was almost dissatisfied with what I was feasting on. I wanted more.

I loved the Word, but when it came to preaching and messages out there, I just felt bored and like I was being handed a salami stick instead of a fat, juicy steak.

I wanted meat. I wanted more. And I desired to hear someone who was eating it and speaking about their real-life experience with our limitless and infinite God.

It sounds judgmental, but I wanted to hear something fresh, not the old manna I kept hearing. Even back then, I was wired to be hungry for the new.

Then I was invited to a meeting where a Canadian revivalist was speaking, so I went along, not knowing what to expect.

The first night he got up and spoke, I could feel the glory in the room even before he said a word, and I knew instantly that he had been with Jesus. Then he started sharing about his encounters and the room felt electric. My hunger only increased. "I want that!" I said to myself.

But what stood out to me was that this guy had a really unique message and voice. Many criticized him and slandered him for what he spoke about, but to me, it was a feast.

I remember hearing him talk about the secret place and the Father's house, and it sent me into years of encounters simply by hungering and making a withdrawal on heaven for the same thing.

I went to bed on the night of the last conference day and went into a dream where that Canadian revivalist was in a spacesuit, telling us how to go into space. I woke up knowing this was the Lord inviting me into deeper encounters and realms of revelation I didn't have at the time.

But what I didn't realize was that beyond encounters, God was inviting me into a lifestyle of being a voice for Him many years later that was okay with being out of the box for the sake of stewarding and living in the realm of visitation and revelation that was unusual for most.

And that's what being a pioneering voice is. It's taking what God is saying and about to do and introducing it to the present and walking it out no matter what it costs and no matter what people think about you for it.

## OWNING YOUR VOICE

Do you believe you are a pioneering voice?

I would never have called myself "a voice" back in the day. I still don't like titles, or any form of label, because I've spent so many years getting used to just being "a son" that they make me feel like I'm polishing myself up better than I am.

But I've had to accept that I am a voice to deliver this to other voices out there who, maybe like me, have never fit a particular box or popular preference.

At the very least, I pray your takeaway from this letter is accepting that, regardless of your doubts and insecurities or what others have said about you, you can't deny that you know in your spirit that you are called to be a voice, too.

Not the kind voice you see tickling the ears of the masses with their perfectly articulated verbiage and emotional tones that draw you in.

Not the kind of voice that makes you feel tucked in for a bedtime story, tenderly and slowly appealing to your soul, but they are trying to buy you into their narrative.

Not the kind of voice that can speak to your comforts and sell you a story of false hope and aspiration.

No, you aren't the TED Talk type. You aren't trying to massage the intellect of a generation.

You are the voice crying out in the wilderness, "Prepare ye the way of the Lord!"

Just like John the Baptist, you are a bit of an oddball. Maybe your calling and passion have branded you as socially awkward and strange because it bursts out of you involuntarily.

But no, you aren't strange. You are just wired authentically.

You don't have the filter they do. You don't have the assistant screening your words before you speak them or cutting out what could offend.

You aren't politically correct. Not that you want to upset any-one, but your spirit connects to your mouth in a way that isn't ac-ceptable in the world of proper, aristocratic prophetic ministry.

Am I speaking to you?

I don't tick all those boxes either—and never have.

## BREAKING IT DOWN

So how do you survive in a hyper-critical world where people are always sizing you up, judging what you say, judging what you don't say, and assuming they know your heart?

How do you begin to steward your voice and maintain being a voice without being cut down and thrown out in the trash in your first week?

How do you stay true to what God is telling you to speak with-out compromising, cutting yourself down to fit, or suppressing yourself to walk the road of least resistance?

How do you be a wild voice in this time of history?

How do you last the distance?

Here are a few practical things God has taught me over the years that will hopefully help you keep being the unique "you" in this hour:

### *YOU HAVE ONE ASSIGNMENT.*

John's assignment was simple: he cleared the way for Jesus. If you don't know your message or assignment, ask God for clarity and begin. Too many voices get stuck in the hesitation stage when they just need to begin. Don't take on too many functions. Just speak what He gives you and let Him do the rest.

### *START WITH WHAT YOU'VE GOT.*

The other thing that stops voices from consistently speaking is feeling like they don't have what it takes. "I don't know how to get the words right. I don't know how to say it like them." Don't let your lack of skill stop you from obeying God. He will always increase your gifts as you step out. This leads me to the next one.

### YOU ARE ONE OF A KIND.

You have to quit comparing yourself to others on social media. I've done it and it sabotages your authentic flavor and message. Your anointing is greatest when you are true to how God designed you, even if it is strange or unique. Trust the way God wired you and refuse to become like everyone else to be liked or to get followers. Just be you and entrust that to God.

### LET GOD GET YOUR MESSAGE OUT.

Stewarding your voice effectively is having to choose not to hide it, but it doesn't mean you have to fall into the trap of thinking you need to be a marketer. Let God get your message out. You don't have to pay for ads or try to network or rub shoulders to get your message out. Just be faithful to release it and He will surprise you with where He takes it. I have seen far too many people pay and hustle their way into notoriety God didn't endorse, and it's a hard job to upkeep the doors you pushed down.

### GET OVER YOURSELF.

Being a voice is not about you, nor is it attached to your reputation. Of course, people don't see it that way, but you have to learn to see it as God's voice through you. When you do that, it helps you speak what He gives you with greater confidence, because it's NOT YOU. So be HIS VOICE on the earth, knowing He backs you.

### LIVE IN THE SECRET PLACE.

Far too many emerging voices start off right. Their message erupts from their wilderness season and soon gains traction, but instead of maintaining their lifestyle of intimacy, they begin to shift into a lifestyle of being around other prophets and leaders instead of staying in the posture that launched them. Stay in the secret place so that you don't run dry and burn out.

## HUNGER FOR FRESH MANNA.

While there is nothing wrong with keeping your message consistent, I do believe God wants us to build upon what we receive. Encounters and visitation lead us to a much deeper revelation of what we received earlier. Like another layer of insight and anointing, fresh manna will keep you fresh and your oil burning. Don't be satisfied with the old, and don't rely on old encounters until you run out of juice. Lean in for the fresh.

## KEEP YOUR VOICE HONEST & PURE.

People ask me, "How much of the revelation you receive from God do you release?" I would say five percent. Revelation is sacred and birthed out of intimacy. To share everything would be violating my relationship with God, or PROSTITUTING the gift. You keep your voice honest and pure by increasing your ability to discern what is for the masses and what is for your history.

## TRADE IN THE ORPHAN SPIRIT.

I used to operate in a major orphan spirit in my teens and early twenties, and it skewed my thinking. It made it impossible for me to work with others and be a voice for the Lord because everything He gave me was filtered through my identity dysfunction. Many emerging voices wrestle with this, and it leads them into a parallel universe of the calling God has for them. It's a thief and robber. It will cause you to post for likes and share words for affirmation. It will cause you to compete and grab for moments in the spotlight. Pioneers, you need to be fathered into a healthy identity. Seek this more than being heard. Seek this more than releasing your sound, so that when you do, it will be pure and powerful to those who hear it.

## DON'T CAST YOUR PEARLS.

A big lesson I wish I had learned early on is that not everyone is for you and your mission. Many only want to get close to you so that they can steal from the fresh flow coming out of you! I remember being so excited when God started speaking through me that I wanted to tell everyone my deepest thoughts and weightiest revelations. I wanted to share all my dreams, new words fresh off the printing press of heaven, and projects and ideas, and what happened? People stole them, used them, and trampled over them. Which leads me to...

## KNOW YOUR COMPANY.

Do you know who labors amongst you? Do you know their hearts and motives? I don't need to elaborate on this one. I have almost thrown in the towel from not paying attention to the red flags that led me to multiple betrayals, slander seasons, and hijacks of my calling. If there is something to pray and fast on, it's to know who your close circle and company are meant to be and who they aren't.

## ALIGNMENTS ARE CONTRACTS.

Recently, I had a few amazing groups contact me wanting to lock arms and run together. The sentiment is humbling, and I know their hearts were probably pure in their desire to run with us, but what I have learned over the years is that alignments are contracts. I have entered into covenants and alignments God never asked me to, and it has always shut down my voice for long periods or diluted it. Supporting other movements is kingdom, but before you give your word or vow about anything deeper, take it into a season of prayer and fasting.

### A SAUL WILL ALWAYS BE WAITING.

When you begin stepping out as a voice, I guarantee you that this will happen: a Saul will present themselves. Who is this Saul? A person is normally a leader or a more seasoned voice that sees what is on your life and either doesn't want you to exceed their level of success or a person who wants to use you to prop up their waning ministry. It happens like clockwork, and it's a deadly trap of flattery and ego-stroking to those new to the game. And when you have been a Lone Ranger for so long, you tend to see this sudden interest as favor and hand over the keys to them all too quickly. Please beware! Protect and guard your anointing. Don't appoint people whom you don't know or God has not spoken to you about.

### LONE RANGER SEASONS DON'T MAKE YOU ILLEGITIMATE.

Not long ago, I had a well-known pastor drag someone under the bus in front of me. He said these pastors were illegitimate because they had no covering from a major church or network. As he spoke, I saw into his heart and saw the gaping fear of losing territory. He didn't like the favor they were getting and had to use the only card he had: to discredit this emerging ministry in a need to further validate his own. Let me say this clearly: Lone Ranger seasons are ordained by God. He uses them to purify and heal us before He launches us in a public way. Don't see them as a bad thing like many do. Covering has become an idol and way of bullying those who are carrying unique messages that would never be approved by the stuck-up clergy of the religious club. If you are a Lone Ranger, know that it's a season God has you in, but keep your heart ready for God to bring you to the right people at the right time instead of the wrong people just to appease their need for you to be legit.

## DON'T PAY ATTENTION TO THE PROPHETIC POLICE.

Another trap many fall into is listening to the prophetic police. I have spent so many years trying to breathe life and courage back into voices who have been through so much wounding from the mainstream, only to see the rise of a pharisaical spirit coming from leaders who should know better. They write posts essentially telling the emerging voices to shut up because they don't know what they are doing. Does a child learn to walk in a day? Did you ride your bike perfectly the first time you rode it? Did the disciples become seasoned overnight? Please disregard the condemnation of these voices who should be stepping into their shoes as fathers/mothers but have failed to do so and have deviated from their calling. No matter what they say, be a voice anyway and let the Father's words over you be the only voice you hear.

## YOU WILL ENCOUNTER JEZEBEL.

I don't want to beat around the bush. You will hit warfare. Regularly. You will have days that are funky and swirly and feel like you are wading through a thick marshland of confusion. Yes, you will face witchcraft, chatter, and chins wagging to pull you down. But the greatest attack will come from the Jezebel spirit. She hates your voice and will try to discredit you and make you feel stupid for speaking at all. She will make you want to run and give up. And she will send her loyal assassins in to do her bidding. Just like the enemy will position a Saul to bring you into a false covenant, she will send one of her representatives in to try to be your best friend and cheer squad, but they will be positioned there to steal your voice. Don't fall for her traps!

## STAY IN YOUR LANE.

There are days you will wake up to the news of chaotic world events, and then the inevitable tsunami of prophetic voices suddenly prophesying, virtue signaling, or reminding you of what they said about it years ago. That's fine for them, but what if God didn't tell you about it? What do you do if the pressure to speak up is mounting, but God has something else on your radar? Don't fall under the pressure to say something simply to appease people or be politically correct. Stay in your lane. If it's not in your lane, don't enter the fight. You can't be everything to everyone. You have to stay within the grace and bounds of your anointing.

## YOU ARE NOT A VENDING MACHINE.

Hear me say this: You are no one's personal prophet. Someone might ask you, "Can you hear God for me because I don't invest in my relationship enough to hear Him for myself?" The moment you agree to that, you can be assured that you will be called upon when they need something from God, but instead, they will demand it from you. You are not their vending machine. You are not a psychic. Refuse to enable people who aren't willing to go after God for themselves. Just so you know my heart, I'm not condemning people who are after a prophetic word. I get dozens of these requests daily from people who have only known a kingdom where they are disempowered from hearing God for themselves. But YOU are not their answer unless God instructs you to.

## YOU HAVE PERMISSION TO BREAK NEW GROUND.

You weren't given your calling to maintain your post but to extend the borders of the kingdom with it. One of the greatest traps many voices fall into is playing it safe. Trying to uphold an image or reputation. Like I said earlier, this isn't about you. You are a dead man. Christ Jesus now lives in you. Please don't play it safe. Be bold. Break new ground. You have been permitted to carve new paths and write new language for the hour. You have been permitted to confront the old and unveil the new, blow away the dross of the past era, and lead the church into something fresh.

## CHOOSE CHARACTER OVER GIFTING.

I prayed years ago, "Lord, never let my anointing or gifting grow bigger than my character," and I would like to think He honored that. My leash has been short and He deals with me regularly. Too many voices fall into the trap of stopping the Lord from developing their character, and it begins to show. Don't ever leave the Potter's hands, because it's the safest place to be.

## STAY A NOVICE.

Pioneers, stay a novice. This means staying humble and small in your own eyes. Don't fall into the trap of feeling invincible because you have tasted ten minutes of favor. Popularity is poison to many voices, but there is a way to have influence while staying small and teachable. I've noticed that those who see God move upon them long-term are those who don't get lost in the fame and fortune of their success. They also don't parade themselves or their revelation like it's the missing link of humanity. Stay a novice.

## LOVE JESUS MORE THAN MINISTRY.

Lastly, don't take yourself too seriously. Don't lose yourself in your mission and forget to be a person with needs, a prosperous soul, and a healthy marriage and family. Pour more time and focus there than you do pouring out. Above all, love Jesus. Don't let ministry become your mistress or idol. Last the distance by stewarding this well. Be normal. Be real. Have hobbies. Laugh. Live with adventure. Be creative. Live for the audience of one.

Emerging voices, you can do this.

*(This list is not conclusive and I feel I could go on forever, but I pray it helps you step out and last the distance.)*

# PIONEERING AGAIN

*Dear Pioneers,*

As we come towards the end of this book, I feel to share about the process we all face after one pioneering season ends and another begins.

Let me dive into it.

Remember the dream I had a few chapters back of the pioneer crossing? I have been pondering that dream again lately.

At the beginning of the year, I had another dream that felt similar where I felt like the Lord was speaking to the church that it was crucial for us right now to break away from the ways and methods we have been operating in and step into something new again.

In fact, it felt like a warning that unless we did pioneer this year in some way we would find ourselves feeling dry, stale, outdated, and expired.

But it was more than that. He showed me that places of comfort can become ceilings that then over time become compromise.

As we crossed over I felt it—the grace period on certain activities, methods, and messages was beginning to wane and God wanted us to dream forward with the Lord.

Then that dreaming turned into an awkward and painful wrestle with the new that felt so obscure and what was clearly changing and ending. It was a difficult balance or dance to maintain.

The other difficulty was trying to reconcile what we expected and what we were seeing. The door we thought we were opening didn't end up being the door that came before us, and the package destiny was wrapped in just felt unfamiliar.

I know you had to see many seeds fall to the ground in the last few years. I know that pain. I know it doesn't feel fair and you still have so many questions unanswered.

I know that you had to close more doors than you opened and leave behind far more than you were picking up.

I know it was a big sacrifice and I know that few understood you for it.

I mean you could have taken that opportunity, that position, that deal, that offer, that much easier way but you wouldn't have felt right.

You could have stayed in that alignment, relationship, and connection but it would have felt like compromise to you.

What people don't understand about you, and maybe you don't yet see either, is that this is not about pioneering to you, although that's the outcome—this is worship.

Like David dancing the ark back to its rightful place and being ridiculed for it. It's your worship.

Like John the Baptist eating, dressing, and speaking differently to get an unusual message across—this is your worship.

And like Elisha slaying his oxen and burning his old tools to go follow the call of God— this is your worship.

And right now all of heaven is cheering you on because you

have said yes to a life of following the Spirit of God where few say yes to go.

Because it's uncomfortable at first. It can be painful. It's harder to navigate because there is no map for it.

But the fruit...the fruit is unlike anything else you will ever see. And it's the fruit that God is so eager for us to see this year.

You were not created to go through the motions. You were not created to tick all the boxes of human possibility, but you were created to be a revealer of the new and the impossible.

Right now the Holy Spirit is BROODING over His church and SEARCHING intently for the ones who are willing to BREAK AWAY from the pack, from the mundane, from the safe...and reveal the new ember burning quietly on the inside of them.

Those willing to pay attention to the still, small voice and fan that flame.

This is a year to pioneer because it is time that the church births what the enemy has been trying to prevent us from birthing!

We have been in a warzone and the target has been our creativity, innovation, strategies, and legacy.

There are songs that need to be written that become the soundtracks of revival that lead us out into open pastures. There are songs that need to come that will be the breakers for those in the church who are STUCK.

There are anthems aching to be sung by a generation that knows they are alive for more than just reacting to and enduring the noise of the news and are awakened to their purpose.

There are books that need to come. The library of heaven is full of books that have not been pulled down to earth. There are ideas and inventions and powerful blueprints that need to come.

As they come, they will become weapons in our hands against the enemy's plans, and we will storm the frontlines as a force to be reckoned with.

As I write this, I see scrolls falling with the words redemption written upon them, and I feel like they are the blueprints of global redemption and restoration. God is giving out assignments today and strategies to turn around that injustice, to solve that problem, and to heal that issue.

Will you receive them? Will you take the path less traveled this year to see the fruit you have been craving to see?

I know you have felt the strange discontent like somehow there was MORE than what you were seeing. This was the Lord giving you the heads up, saying, "I am changing your appetite because I have something remarkable around the corner."

And where you have spent a year burying dreams and desires and feeling so heartsick from the ending of an era of your life, this will be a year of LIFE & PLANTING THE NEW.

But what is this all for? Pioneers are those who break the church OUT of stagnant places and bondage and break us INTO places of blessing and breakthrough.

They are the ones who charge through the smokescreens and invite us into the new landscape.

They bring a new language never spoken and print the news heaven is speaking.

They are the brokers of the fresh spring and the NOW word of the Lord—hot on the pulse of where the Holy Spirit is moving.

*"For those who are led by the Spirit of God are the children of God" (Romans 8:14).*

And I hear Him saying, "Will you come?"

Let's go back to go forward. Let's get low to go higher. Let's lay down our plans to pick up something better.

Leave the last few years behind. Ask Him to refresh you and let's begin!

## QUESTIONS TO ASK GOD THAT WILL HELP YOU PIONEER

- What is Your hand on?
- What is it not upon anymore?
- What are You doing?
- Where are You moving?
- What are the themes on Your heart?
- What songs are being sung in heaven?
- Where do You want me this year?
- What do You want me to do?
- What path do You have me on?
- Who are my people?
- What are the new strategies and ideas in Your heart for me to carry?

## DANGEROUS PIONEER PRAYERS

- Lord, have Your way in me.
- I'll go wherever You ask me to go.
- I surrender my old operating system to You.
- I surrender my activities and assignments.
- Give me only Your activities and assignments
- Take me deeper with You.
- Show me the path You want me to walk on.
- Shut the door to avenues that are robbing me.
- Shut the door to people and places that are keeping me from moving with You.
- Remove any and all complacency from my life.
- Give me dreams and encounters that wreck me for the ordinary.
- Use me.
- Anoint me.
- Fill me in Jesus' name.

## THERE'S A NEW GO COMING!

Pioneers, we have been in a time of deep surrender and a threshing floor moment for us personally and the church as we hand over the keys and reins to a past way of Christian life and kingdom.

We have had to take our hands off the old plow and burn our old tools and oxen. We have had to give God the deeds to what we have built for decades.

For some this is just a heart posture and re-focus of vision, but for many it's a letting go of a whole world we created.

We have been in a time where suddenly it seemed as if God changed His mind on some of the things we were doing and building; however, it's not the full picture. God has been wanting us to simply give Him what's in our hands so that He can tweak and upgrade our vision.

The building plans are being overhauled, the infrastructure is being modified and strengthened, and God is wanting us to partner with Him in His new focus for this next chapter we are heading into.

As I am writing this down I just heard, "There is INCREASE in the ADJUST!" Where you have had to change your plans to accommodate God's plans, you will find an ease and grace you didn't have.

The hustle has to end. The push and the fight have to come to an end so that this next chapter is in the fresh flow of the Spirit and not in your own flesh anymore.

## FROM THE FLOOR TO THE OPEN DOOR

Recently I had a vision of an open door that was waiting for people to enter it. It reminded me of the door in Revelation 4:1:

*"After this I looked, and there before me was a door standing open in heaven. And the voice I had first heard speaking to me like a trumpet said, "Come up here, and I will show you what must take place after this."*

It was a door that would transport us from the threshing floor season we have been in to a new day.

It was the shift from survival and sorrow to revelation and wonder.

It was the turning of the corner from extreme loss and the end to a vision, to the revealing of the new plans, blueprints, and new purpose.

## THE NEXT CHAPTER

What is this period of time? I believe it's another cycle of pioneering the new.

That's right, pioneering the new. But haven't we already been pioneering? We have been. We have been readying for this next chapter.

Recently, I heard the Lord simply say, "There is a new GO coming."

What is this GO? It's the go of the gospel. It's the commissioning of those who have felt stuck and grounded being released and sent out again in new assignments.

*"He said to them, "Go into all the world and preach the gospel to all creation" (Mark 16:15).*

The word "GO" here means to depart, make passage, and shift out from the place you have been in.

It means that this temporal holding pattern many have been in is coming to an end. Its purpose has been to de-clutter us from the past season and break us out of the mindsets of that paradigm.

It's also been a heart and wound healing season as God revisits the places of pain and hope deferred from the last pioneering season and prepares us for the new wineskin season we are heading into.

It means that the stuck place you have been in—unable to see forward or know what decision to make is coming to an end, and your next steps are going to be made clear.

And I feel this so deeply—God is going to finish what He started in you! This was not a cancellation of the call or the vision. God will honor His word and bring it to completion!

## THE NEW GO BRINGS THE GREEN LIGHT

- The GO is the green light where last week things were still not adding up. Over the next few months, doors will start to open again.
- It's the green light of heaven where all roads have been blocked.
- The GO brings the green light, favor, and provision.
- The GO is a breaker that supersedes all natural and man-made obstacles, defying red tape, and breaking through places not humanly possible.
- The GO brings new company, alignments, and tribe.
- The GO ignites fresh passion, zeal, and a new message.
- The GO shatters the muzzle the enemy tried to silence you with.
- The GO unlocks revelation and new themes and language from heaven for the road ahead.
- The GO is a fresh mantle, anointing, and unction to operate in something new you haven't before.
- The GO is the Lord anointing you afresh in front of your enemies and handing you a new baton.

## A GO PRAYER OVER YOU

So I feel in my spirit to pray for you as you transition out of GROUNDING to GOING. I pray that this season of internal rewiring and heart reset will finish its process in and through you, and for the old patterns and cycles to be handed over. I pray for healing and deliverance over you right now and for the power of the Spirit to rest upon you, brooding over you as you bring this season to a close. Now I prophesy for the doors to swing wide open, for the dots to connect, and for every single thing to line up in Jesus' name. Lord refresh them, and set them up for the greatest GO they have seen in their lives in Jesus' name!

## FOR THOSE IN A PAUSE, GET READY FOR YOUR MARCHING ORDERS!

Now lastly, let me speak to those who have been in the pause season after your last pioneering season ended.

Over the last few days, I kept hearing the Lord say, "I am giving my marching orders."

I believe this is the Lord. Handing out strategic and specific instructions to those who've been waiting on their next steps and the things that the Lord is asking them to step into.

These are the instructions for those who've been patiently waiting and not rushing ahead of the Lord to receive only what He has to give, and refusing to step into hustle or their own strength.

These orders are for those who have their ear to the ground and have been longing to hear what the Lord is leading them into in this next season.

I really felt this was for those specifically who've been in a season of waiting and pause, those who were in a time of being refreshed, refueled, healed, and yet ready to embark on new orders again.

There are also so many who have been shipwrecked by circumstances, sickness, and financial setbacks that God is going to stand back to their feet.

The other side of this is I felt like the marching orders also represented what the Lord was leading His people out of.

Since January, there's been a strong sense of closure that's come upon the body of Christ. Where the Lord has been leading people out of wrong alignments and old wineskin assignments and activities.

I believe in May and June we're going to see many of those alignments wrapped up and finalized.

We're going to see many people leave many environments and habitats that they've been occupying for a long period of time, and the Lord will move them into a new sphere of influence and even location.

This will be a time when He changes your title, your role, and your desk nameplate.

This is a time when He changes your clothes and your name and then leads you into a wider open space that He's been preparing for you.

Watch as God begins moving people out of positions and places that they have not stewarded correctly or properly.

I don't believe this is a condemnation word over those in the body of Christ, but more for those who've been deliberately moving against the Lord and moving against what the Spirit of the Lord is doing.

In saying that, I believe this is also an hour governmentally, where the Lord is going to shift and move people out of places of authority that were never given by the Lord but were given by man. This is a time of great exposure in governmental realms. In places where people have been in roles and places that do not carry the heart of the Lord and the Spirit of God, now is the time when

God will actually usher those who carry His heart and will steward them correctly into these roles.

This is a time right now when the Lord is giving His marching orders to His remnant, to His pioneers, those who have His heart, and those who represent Him well. He is leading them into a time of expansion and increase.

I specifically just want to say yet again to those who have been in a pause and a waiting season, get ready because the Lord is about to reposition you. Look for the strategic and acute insight that He's about to pour out that leads you into fresh clarity for what He has ahead for you.

For I hear the Spirit of the Lord saying, "Am I a God of confusion? For you have had many seductive voices surrounding you, leading you into confusion and chasing you to doubt Me or the promises I have given you. Will I not do it?"

And even now the Lord is releasing the Issachar anointing upon the church so that she is able to DISCERN the kairos we are in and know how to plan and walk it out practically. Receive it today!

Your marching orders are coming because we are in a governmental shift in the body of Christ, out of powerlessness and into a militant occupation in the earth.

You may feel defeated on the battlefield, but I prophesy to you in the name of Jesus to stand to your feet, dust yourself off, and begin to tie up your boots because the Lord is calling you into a season of renewed strength and vision in Jesus' name!

*"I will instruct you and teach you in the way which you should go; I will counsel you with My eye upon you."*—Psalms 32:8

Pioneers, you are entering a fresh season of new exploits for the Lord!

# THE REDEMPTION TOUR

*Dear Pioneers,*

After the last letter, I felt I needed to prophesy and speak to those who know that, just as I shared, there is a new GO coming, but they just may feel a little critical or less hopeful about it.

If that was you...I get it. Trust me.

I felt such a stirring to share what I believe the Lord is doing right now in so many pioneers who have felt hope deferred and soul-sick for a long period of time.

I'm talking about those who've walked through hardship after hardship, breakdown after breakdown, and train wreck after train wreck after following the Lord on the unpopular path.

Maybe the word *redemption* to you at this point feels too good to be true and you feel slightly critical if it's even mentioned. If so, then this is for you. Let's watch God break off some deep disappointment.

I feel like I'm speaking to those who, at the height of promises, dreams, and what they felt like was a birthing, suddenly came into calamity, ruin, and failure.

Yes, I'm speaking to those who've had their hopes dashed and have been living in disappointment and survival mode for many years. I feel that to release this properly, I need to be vulnerable and share a bit of our story with you.

## THE INTERRUPTED PROMISE

Leading up to 2020, God gave us multiple dreams about major promises over our lives, and as you may know, we moved and gave up everything to follow the Lord without a thought.

In March 2020, we arrived in the United States following a specific dream to come on a certain date. Our goal was to purchase a ministry home ready for our arrival later in the year when our visas were approved. But then COVID hit and we were stuck, and we watched as each of those dreams suddenly folded before our eyes.

We lost the home we were supposed to purchase and were essentially strangers in the land we felt was home.

## WATCHING SEEDS FALL TO THE GROUND

By the end of 2021, we had to finalize our visas, so we went back to Australia with our tail between our legs, feeling like we'd failed and that we hadn't heard from the Lord.

Upon arriving, we were escorted by the Australian federal police to a quarantine facility in Sydney, where we spent two weeks there just wondering what we'd done wrong and why all these promises hadn't come to pass. To make matters worse, they almost didn't let us leave, because they lost one of our tests on the final day, which meant they wanted to keep us in there for another 14 days.

Thanks to Christy's fiery, "There's no way we are staying in your scamdemic prison another day longer!" and with the great help of the head of police for that area, who came to our rescue, we were able to leave.

Then we spent most of 2022 watching the last fragments of all of these dreams fall like seeds to the ground and die. And what was worse, it even felt like the Lord was asking us, "Will you give them to Me? Will you surrender all of them to Me?" And we did. But then the big one: God asked us to lay down our visas altogether. So we did.

We walked through grief and deep sorrow as we gave them to the Lord and placed them in His lap, then let Him refresh and re-fuel us, and He did. Grief began to turn to a deeper abandon, and then abandon into worship, and worship into freedom and delight again. Our slate was wiped clean. We had no chips or cards on the table, just our family and Jesus.

## THE WINDS OF CHANGE & SUDDEN DOORS

Then something shifted. Suddenly, God was beginning to resurrect some of these dreams rapidly, and by October, it was like we were watching every one of those seeds being picked up and the Holy Spirit was blowing upon them afresh.

Somehow, the season of surrender and laying down was doing more than we realized. We were suddenly dreaming afresh, receiv-ing downloads in a new way, and feeling a second wind.

Mind you, this is where the warfare really amped up. Everyone around us started saying, "Forfeit the USA! Stay in Australia!" It was confusing, to say the least. I had already given it up, but I was waking up every night at 3 a.m. in cold sweats, weeping over the United States. The war was real, but something had shifted.

Then it happened. God suddenly opened a door and we found ourselves holding the very promise that felt so far away and impos-sible a year earlier.

## THE WORD THAT CHANGED EVERYTHING

So we packed up, and in early January, we flew to Sydney en route to the US to officially begin our migration, but when we arrived, many of the hotels in that area were booked out.

The only hotel that was available happened to be the very hotel that we'd stayed in for quarantine. "No way," I thought and showed Christy.

"Is this a joke? Is God trying to tease us with this? Why would we have to stay in this hotel the night before we fly back to America? Was this a sign that everything was going to crumble again? Was this a sign that we were going to see further hope deferred and watch these very dreams that God had suddenly resurrected fall to the ground yet again? Were we leading our family through another season of heartache and trauma?"

As we drove to the hotel, we stepped out into the lobby and had the eerie recollection of watching the nurses and federal police escort us out on our last day. I looked over at Christy and she looked over at me. Suddenly, I heard the voice of the Lord speak so clearly: "Nate, this is not what you think it is. I'm taking you on a redemption tour."

As we got into our hotel room, we prayed and took communion as a family. I could see it on my kids' faces: "What's happening? Why are we here again 13 months later?" But that night, we had the best sleep we had in what felt like years.

The next day, as we went to the airport to fly out, we still had a lot of fears hanging over us and were still walking through the process of what we had just endured these last few years.

Yet I had this word embedded deep in my heart: "You're on a redemption tour."

## THE LAST ATTEMPT TO DERAIL US

Then as we cleared ticketing and security, I started receiving messages and emails. Somehow, all our personal bank accounts had been hacked, our websites crashed, and we had no money to even eat before the flight. But we just laughed it off. We were on the road of redemption and the enemy was mad.

But upon arriving in the United States, we were let off the plane to stand in immigration for over four hours, which isn't uncommon, but strangely, we were led to an interrogation room where we were questioned about our status.

We were not told why we were there except that we may have to wait up to 12 hours to hear whether they were going to let us in or send us back to Australia. I started to feel that familiar feeling of, "I knew this was too good to be true, this redemption tour," when suddenly I remembered a word a friend had given me only a month earlier about how he saw two large angels standing with us that were going to break open the way because the enemy was going to try to stop us.

And then the Lord took me back to March 2020, when we arrived in San Francisco, and I physically saw two angels with the Scripture, Isaiah 45:1-3, written on the side of them as we entered through immigration and into the United States.

Wow. Those two angels had not left our side. They'd been there ever since. So Christy, the kids, and I dropped to the floor and prayed, "Lord, break open the way!"

Instantly, our names were called and they said, "We have no idea why we brought you in here, but you could have been in there for 12 hours!" They let us go, and it was as if those two angels busted open that door and released us. We were home!

## THE ROAD OF FULL CIRCLE CIRCUMSTANCES & DO-OVERS

Now we have been here in the United States for a year now, and I can attest to this: God has been faithful and we have indeed been on the road to redemption.

It's as if He has intentionally led us to places and situations that were literal do-overs from the season of barrenness and robbery.

We have found ourselves in full-circle moments that had my head spinning about how God orchestrated it.

We have seen every single area of hope deferred begin to come alive and resurrected again.

We've seen every single dream that looked like it'd fallen to the ground restored, and we've seen the years that the locusts had eaten begin to be recovered.

But this isn't just a cool story. I feel like what we have been going through is not just for us either.

I believe that what we have been going through is a prophetic picture of what the church has been walking through, what you have been walking through. The hope deferred, the disappointments, the dead seeds, the pain, the heartache, the loss, and the trauma.

But let me prophesy over you the same words that God spoke over me: Pioneers, you are on a redemption tour, in Jesus' mighty name!

I prophesy that the place that you've been stuck in, and the experiences and the circumstances that have been dealt to you, is not what you're going to end up with.

You are on a redemption tour and it begins now, in Jesus' mighty name.

I pray that in the area of health—redemption now!

I just decree in the name of Jesus over your finances—redemption!

Over your hopes and dreams and destiny—redemption!

Over your relationships—redemption!

Over your family and marriages—redemption in the mighty name of Jesus!

I command every area that the enemy has eaten and stolen, it must now come back and be restored to you.

And I decree this and prophesy this over you—robbery ends this week and redemption begins in the mighty name of Jesus!

*"I will repay you for the years the locusts have eaten—the great locust and the young locust, the other locusts and the locust swarm, my great army that I sent among you. You will have plenty to eat, until you are full, and you will praise the name of the Lord your God, who has worked wonders for you; never again will my people be shamed" (Joel 2:25-26).*

*Letter Twenty-One*

# ASCEND THE MOUNTAIN

*Dear Pioneers,*

Recently, I wrote a yearly prophetic word, but I felt that this word was not just for a year, but a timestamp for the remnant before the return of Jesus.

I felt it was a needed heart shift for a pioneering people called to "prepare the way of the Lord" and a clear directive of how to finish well in the days to come. So I feel it's only right to put my pen down after this chapter and call you into the very commissioning of this word.

I've been asking the Lord since August what our posture should be for the next year and the years to come. I could sense the holiness around it and the caution not to approach it like any other year. Then, in September, I began to feel a sudden and massive internal shift. It started with a deep discontent, and then I began having nonstop dreams about the same thing: ascending the mountain to be with Jesus.

It's consumed me for months now: a longing to break away from the norm, from the hustle and bustle and be with Him. What if God was preparing us for something we can only step into by lying down? What if God was leading the church into a season of increase of our authority, breakthrough, and dominion that can only come by stepping into being "seated in Christ in heavenly places" (Ephesians 2:6)?

Bill Johnson says, "There are lovers and workers, and lovers will always get more work done than the workers."

What if we are entering a Psalm 24 season whereby, ascending the hill of the Lord, we break away from the last remnants of man's institution and methods and begin to operate from a vantage point of victory we have never known?

What if God was calling us to leave behind the busyness of ministry and enter the priesthood of Samuel once again, that will accomplish so much more?

What if this discontent was a DIVINE INTERRUPTION to reveal the old manna and lead us into the new? This is what is burning in my heart more profoundly than I can express, and I pray you catch it.

One night recently, I woke up hearing the Lord speak about the coming year, and so I want to share what I heard in bullet point form:

## A 'GOING UP THE MOUNTAIN' SEASON

I heard the Lord say,

- I am breaking you away from the rat race that has worn you down and exhausted you.
- I am leading you away from the rest of the herd, not to isolate you but to free you.
- For I have been preparing you to close the door on man's ways and methods that have spread you thin so that you can enter the door of My Spirit.

- I am leading you into a "going up the mountain season," where you will ascend with Me and learn a new rhythm and synergy in My presence.
- It will be a season of coming up the mountain and receiving, then returning down the hill and releasing it to the world.
- Next year, will you give yourself more to the secret place than the public space?
- Will you choose the carpet over the stages?
- Will you come and be poured into more than you pour out?
- Will you lay down your ambitions and ideas and trade them for Mine?
- Will you not rush the special moments that come?
- For up the mountain, I will give you new eyes and a new way of seeing.
- I will give you a heart after My own heart, and you will feel what I feel.
- And you will move in step with Me instead of against Me.
- But be prepared, because this posture will ruin your plans and make you look lazy and foolish, for while others are choosing the hamster wheel, you will choose to sit at My feet.
- It will sometimes feel counter-productive, but I will accomplish far more through you as you choose to ascend.
- And from the mountain, I will reveal My heart and plans to you and invite you into them for the days to come.

## BREAKING NEW GROUND

- Will you break new ground with Me?
- Will you choose what I am doing other than what the masses are calling "kingdom"?
- Will you do it My way?

- Will you build what looks foolish to the wise for a season?
- Will you speak the language I give you, even when most don't understand?
- Are you okay with confronting religious norms and "stuck in the mud" ways, even if people disassociate from you?
- Will you leave the areas and roles keeping you in a rut?
- Will you speak what I ask you to speak, even if it makes you look strange, arrogant, or undignified?
- Will you rebuild My temple, My people, My fallen altar (2 Chronicles 24)?
- Will you prioritize My presence and build a place for Me to come (Acts 7:49)?

## LIVING ABOVE THE SNAKE LINE

- You have spent the last three years fighting in the trenches, but you can't do that any longer.
- My church has been lost in the swirl of culture, battling with their hands and intellect instead of My Spirit.
- Second heaven battles have worn you down because I never called you to battle there. Come up higher and learn to wage war from the mountain!
- You have taken hits you didn't need to take and been wounded over and over by engaging in fights I never called you to.
- It's by being seated in ME in heavenly places that you are victorious.
- It's through the finished work of the cross and My blood that you are undefeatable.
- So in this season, I am teaching you how to come up higher where nothing can touch you.
- You will ascend above the chatter and witchcraft and no longer hear the voices or be affected by their curses.

- Yes, you will ascend above the snake line, where you have been battling these assignments endlessly for years.
- For it's time to get back your air superiority and rise above the enemy's games.
- And you will wage war effectively and no longer be disabled by the enemy.
- And as you ascend the hill, you will soon find that all that stuck to you in the past season will come unstuck.
- You will find that all that was attached to you will be detached.
- You will begin to feel a freedom you haven't felt in years as I remove the bondage from your shoulders.
- The fatness and anointing will break all yokes.
- Yes, as you ascend, I will deliver you, heal you, and purify you.
- All bitterness in your heart and flies in the ointment will be removed.
- I am cleaning the hands of My bride so that they can come up and out of the pit they have camped in for far too long.
- And all Baals will be purged from their lips.
- For I am done with hearing mixture from the pulpit and seeing My bride celebrating the compromise of culture.
- This season, I am purifying and delivering My church so that they will be, again, set apart unto Me.
- In 2024, there will be an anointing to distinguish good from evil, and they will become apparent to those who ascend.
- I will expose the enemy's plans on the world stage and call My ascended ones to counteract them.
- I will expose the hands of the wicked and thwart the plans of the crafty so that their plans achieve no success.

## EVEN MORE SET APART

- For in this season, I am setting you even more apart.
- This doesn't mean I am isolating you further or leading you into a lonely season. Still, you will notice that I intentionally separate you from those unwilling to ascend.
- You will notice this quickly, for I am a jealous and protective God, and I don't want you continuing to cast your pearls and have your heart trampled on by people who aren't for you.
- This is why I have been leading you away from the pack.
- I have been putting a distaste in your mouth for the appetite of the elites and Sauls.
- I have been giving you discernment to see where people have been in bed with Jezebel and choosing divination over what can only be acquired by intimacy with Me.
- Your eyes will be opened even more as you ascend.
- But I am leading you to a company that is not just friends but a covenant family.
- And I will knit your hearts together because you have chosen Me above the masses.

## THE ALTARS OF DECISION & THE CHANGE OF THE GUARD

- For the years to come will be years where there will be a changing of the guard that will be public, but it will first start with the testing of hearts and the crossroads of decision.
- For I am releasing My church into a time of decision: Will they ascend or will they stay in a multitude of noise?
- Will they come up higher or stay in their momentary comforts?
- Will they chase their kingdom or Mine?

- Will they pursue Me and My Word or the affections of people and their shaky foundations?
- Will they leave the hustle and enter My rest?
- Will they untie from the tainted and let go of what is evil?
- Will they choose My altar instead of the altar of Baal?
- The lure of the world is increasing, but I am calling My church to draw a line in the sand and surrender all idols at the altar.
- The change of the guard will be a shock for many, for I am not speaking of a change of assignments but the demotion of the unfaithful and the promotion of the faithful that will come in mid to late 2024.
- For I shall give My glory to those who will steward it well.
- "Lift your heads, oh you gates, swing wide you everlasting doors!"
- In this hour, I am causing My people to LIFT THEIR HEADS!
- I am bringing their gaze UP and back onto Me, for instead, their gaze has been on the problem.
- They have been looking down and inward instead of up and OUT.
- But I am now breaking the hope deferred and heaviness that has been resting on My people, keeping them soul-sick and twisted inside.
- They have been disabled and fractured, but I am leading them into a season of chiropractic realignment of soul.
- And your heart will come alive again.
- And you will leave the place of deep brokenness and survival weariness.
- So watch now as you lift your head, for you will see My glory rest upon you and rearrange inside you to a degree that will transfigure you.

- People will be able to tangibly see My glory upon your life, and they will say, "Weren't they broken down and burnt out?"
- But My glory will turn you into a new being.
- It will revive you and resurrect you.
- And as My glory comes upon your life, you will become a double doorway for My double glory to be released upon the earth.
- "Swing wide, you heavenly gates, and let the King of Glory in!"
- And My Glory will break off the fear and torment chasing you.
- And My Glory will unlock your voice.
- And My glory will unleash a whole new realm of visitation, revelation, and innovation.
- And My glory will wrap you up like a blanket, and you will finally step into your odyssey for the kingdom.

## LIVING ABOVE THE STORMS & RESTFUL INCREASE

- My bride, I am calling you to live above the storms!
- Storms are only increasing on the earth, but you are called not to be tossed around with them but to live safely above them.
- This is why you must step out of the battlefield of the second heavens and come up to this higher vantage point.
- I am leading you into a season where the tension will become more significant.
- For you will see the hand of the enemy and have to choose to stay seated in Me so that you can correctly navigate and discern the hour.
- For in the midst of chaos, I have ordained for you to flourish.

- In the midst of crisis, I will cause you to remain safe and untouched.
- I have ordained for you to advance and increase in a time when it doesn't make sense for you to.
- For you are not tethered to man's system but to My kingdom.
- I am a problem-solving God, and as you rest in Me, I will protect you from messes, lead you around pits and traps, and hide you under My wings.
- I have not designed for you to live swayed by the storms of the world but to still them.
- And so, in this season, I am calling you to a greater level of faith and multiplication, which you will need to ascend to see what I see and expand your vision and path accordingly.
- And I will give you wisdom to know where to walk and what to do.
- I will give you dreams and revelation to help you grow and multiply when it doesn't make sense to.
- And you will be a marker and a sign for those who have lost their altitude and faith in Me.
- You will be a sign and wonder as they see you settled and stable during increased shaking.
- You will step out of RECESSION and into RECOMPENSE!
- And you will finally see what has been locked up and released to you.
- You will finally see that which has been reserved for this hour given into your hands.
- And you will not only birth, but you will have multiple births to make up for the years the locust ate.

## LIFT UP YOUR HEADS, YOU GATES!

- It's time for My people to be conduits of My glory!
- The days of the glory-less church are over, and this season, I am revealing My bright, shining church that will light up the darkness!
- In this era, My church will no longer be lukewarm, hiding My glory under a basket, but will introduce Me to a world desperate for My power!
- So lift your heads and swing wide your doors and let Me in!
- And My glory will reveal what is hidden and expose the enemy's plans.
- And My glory will purify what is unclean and fix what is broken.
- And My glory will reconnect what has been disconnected.
- And My glory will take back what has been stolen.
- All the gold is Mine, and the silver is Mine, says the Lord, and I shall take back the finance mountain.
- And I shall take back the government mountain and evict the imposters.
- And I shall take back all the mountains that now stand menacing before you.
- So it's time to ascend, My bride, and as you ascend the mountain, you will take back the mountains!

# IF YOU BUILD IT, THEY WILL COME

*Dear Pioneers,*

As I write this last letter, I'm sitting outside on our back porch in the snow and minus ten-degree weather of wintery Colorado.

Just over a year ago, I remember sitting outside in our temporary house in Australia in the hundred-degree heat just about to embark on our move to the USA, and I was feeling so much change swirling around us.

I came to the realization today that I don't think we have ever done anything without crazy risk and faith. To be honest, I have many times envied people who have had the luxury of having everything they needed—the people, the finance, and the blueprint—but for us, it's just never been that way.

The thing with pioneering is that people tend to see your highlight reels but not your messy journey. But I guess one of the purposes of this book is to show you the raw and honest snapshot. I hope I have done that well.

When we were stuck in the US in 2020, my friend Kat surprised me on my birthday by taking me fishing at Lake Shasta. We fished the deeper waters for hours in the boat with no catches or even bites.

So we decided to explore somewhere we hadn't been before, and we came to a place called Dark Canyon. We instantly got stuck because the water was so low, but we persevered and, to our shock, started catching fish!

This has been my experience my whole life. The real fruit is never found in the expected or the safe. It's found when you risk it all and step out in faith.

As we were taking the boat back to shore later that day, Kat said something that shook me to my core. "I don't know anyone who has risked more than you for the kingdom or paid a higher price, but I also don't know anyone with as much fish to show for it as you."

It struck me so deeply. This was 2020, and while churches were closing down, we had thrived, and we were able to be massive givers to those around us, even our students who didn't have food to put on the table.

I was overwhelmed by this reality. The fruit was overflowing. Testimonies of healing and lives transformed were all around us.

But then the tension came into view. What tension?

At that very moment in our lives, we were battling for our visas. It looked bleak. We had chosen the faith journey and we had to choose to look through the eyes of our spirit and at the fruit and not at the circumstances.

What am I getting at? Faith looks stupid if you don't have it. It looks foolish.

We have lost more friends and people simply by being obedient to God than anything else.

Faith doesn't make sense. But it does pay off.

But what if the promise doesn't come when it's meant to? You know our story. God's timing is different from ours.

I didn't want to have to go back to Australia in 2021 and wrestle visas anymore. But we went back on a mission we didn't understand.

The baby you are meant to birth isn't on your timeline, but God's.

## BUY THE FIELD

There is a general in the body of Christ called Lou Engle, who I believe is one of the greatest modern-day pioneers.

This man and his wife Therese started ministry in their forties after decades of burning and travail over America, and they have since started hundreds of movements they have passed on to others to run with, hosted thousands of events, including coliseums and stadiums, and been personally responsible, I believe, for the overturning of Roe v. Wade in 2022.

This is a guy who gathered a million men on the Washington Mall in 2000 to cry out to God. This is a guy who carries a rare burning for things no one else will take and a guy who keeps choosing Jesus over popularity.

He sent a team to DC 18 years ago to pray, and they decided to stay, and the JHOP community was birthed, a community of prayer to see Roe v. Wade overturned. And they accomplished their mission.

And now here we are in 2024, helping Lou plan for a mass gathering of Esthers on the mall in October—Atonement Day—but I have something amazing to share that will astound you.

Recently in the planning of this movement, we hit some obstacles we didn't know how to overcome. We had a big decision to make regarding timing and vision when Christy woke up with a startling dream at 5:55 a.m. to hear a voice say, "If you build it, they will come!" Three times (as I shared earlier in the book).

That morning, she sent her dream to Lou, and he drove around to our house right away. "Do you know my story?" he asked emphatically. "No, we don't," she replied.

Lou began to share how the movie *Field of Dreams* was a prophetic sign for him over the years. He even took his family there to the location in Iowa.

He went on to explain that in every major movement, he has always had a random person show up prior to the event to say, "If you build it, they will come!"

And so that day, prophetic promise and faith erupted in a new fire to move forward, confident in God's provision and power behind us no matter what it looked like.

This is what buying the field looks like. It doesn't make sense, but to the pioneer, it's the only way forward.

And pioneer, you can't keep fighting it. This is your only way forward.

I can't tell you that I have seen the full picture of the pioneering journey, but I can tell you that I know that without faith, it's not pioneering.

Faith pleases God. Pioneering is worship to Him.

To see you "buy the field," whatever that means to you, is like a kiss.

It's you laid down at His feet.

Now that I have shared that, I need to end this book with a word of encouragement and faith over you from a moment of revelation I had with the Lord recently. But before I do, let me ask you a few questions.

## GOD IS GIVING YOU FAITH EYES

What is your field you need to buy?

Do you see this season for what it really is? Can you look through the smoke and fog to see what is really unfolding?

Do you see the door of hope or the door of death and finality?

Do you see the tension and pain or the birthing that is happening?

The Lord would say to you, "Right now, I am releasing eyes of faith to see this moment the way I see it so that those pursuing the uncommon promise do not lose hope!"

## A HALLMARK OF FAITH MOMENT

Recently, I heard the Lord say, "This is a hallmark of faith moment," but I didn't know what that meant. A hallmark is a stamp marking something's genuine properties of purity, and many have been through a season of blind faith and obedience, and God is stamping them with His hallmark.

The hallmark is the branding of heaven upon God's faithful who have been through the refiner's fire and through the valley of darkness. It's the mark of those who have navigated never-ending wildernesses, loss, isolation, and persecution, and pressed on despite only seeing the opposite of the promise they had believed for.

This is a moment that I believe all of heaven is celebrating those who have continued to press through for their families, even though the journey has been rough and unforgiving, and it's a moment of graduation and transition from believing to seeing and from pursuing to beholding.

## THE FULLNESS OF FAITH:
## YOU ARE GOING TO SEE IT WITH YOUR OWN EYES!

Hebrews 11 is known as "the hall of faith," because it speaks of the heroes, the pioneers, and the forerunners that have gone before us. They were the ones who moved, migrated, and left all on a word from the Lord, and God calls them the heroes of faith.

> *"Faith motivated Abraham to obey God's call and leave the familiar to discover the territory he was destined to inherit from God. So he left with only a promise and without even knowing ahead of time where he was going, Abraham stepped out in faith. He lived by faith as an immigrant in his promised land as though it belonged to someone else. He journeyed through the land living in tents with Isaac and Jacob who were persuaded that they were also co-heirs of the same promise. His eyes of faith were set on the city with unshakable foundations, whose architect and builder is God himself. Sarah's faith embraced God's miracle power to conceive even though she was barren and was past the age of childbearing, for the authority of her faith rested in the One who made the promise, and she tapped into his faithfulness"* (Hebrews 11:8-11).

What has been stirred in my spirit for the pioneers in this pinnacle moment is that you are about to SEE the fulfillment with your own eyes! People have called you foolish and stupid for holding on beyond hope, but why do you hold on? Because God has deposited a rare quality in you, a stubborn faith that can't be moved even in times when you wanted it to, and now you will see it established! Read what Hebrews 11:40 says:

"But now God has invited us to live in something better than what they had—faith's fullness! This is so that they could be brought to finished perfection alongside of us."

## FAITH UNLOCKS INEVITABLE MULTIPLICATION

In the months to come, God is going to stir you in a way you haven't felt in years. It will feel like a river is beginning to swell and break the banks of your heart, and you won't be able to contain it.

It will be like a fresh mighty wave building on the inside of you that you cannot hold back or hide. It's the wave of the Spirit of God that He gave you at the beginning of this journey to run with. Once just a tiny swell, now through agitation, the process has become a formidable force for the kingdom.

It's your movement. Maybe small and insignificant at first, but it's building and something has shifted in the battle. Your movement has multiplied, too, and soon you will see it impact the earth publicly and globally and go beyond what you could have done with it.

Your raw faith steps have produced this. Following Jesus has created this.

You said yes and He poured out the bowls of heaven upon it, and now you will see what has looked hidden and foolish to the world become a mighty giant for the kingdom of heaven.

Your movement is about to MULTIPLY.

Even now, God is downloading new plans, fresh vision for it, and establishing connections and pathways you couldn't have orchestrated. Soon it is going to burst the banks, and you'll need to know what to do with it because God knows He can trust you with it.

Like a puzzle, God is using you as a major player and piece for this time of history and for the harvest at hand. Soon you and others will see the full picture and measure of what this looks like.

You once moved with it obediently, but you are about to move with it strategically. You once saw it as an overflow of your worship, but soon you will see that your worship has created an apostolic movement that is going to impact nations.

Get ready for fresh downloads and visions that will confront the outdated methods, and start to expire the ways you are operating. God is giving you the building plans for the next five years and a vision that will require another huge jump of faith to step into it. But it's already in you, and God has already cleared the way.

Pioneers, this is what you were born for. You aren't alone. Keep trekking forward, because your life will be a sign and a wonder of God's goodness to all who see.

NATE JOHNSTON is a prophetic voice and worshiper who has a heart to see sons and daughters unleashed into passionate friendship with God and an effective supernatural lifestyle. His burning cry and desire is to see the Body of Christ become a beacon for the lost by raising up a generation that walks in the love and power of God, representing Him well. Nate and his wife Christy have three daughters, Charlotte, Sophie, and Ava and live in Colorado.

# DISCUSSION QUESTIONS
## FOR GROUP AND PERSONAL REFLECTION

## LETTER 1

- Reflect on the concept of "holy discontent" introduced in the chapter. How can feelings of dissatisfaction or discomfort in your current season be a sign of God calling you to something new? Can you identify a time in your life when this might have been true?

- The chapter discusses David's discontent and his response to Goliath as part of his calling. What lessons can we learn from David's courage and obedience despite his outward limitations? How does his story encourage you to face your own "giants"?

- The metaphor of new wine in new wineskins (Matthew 9:16-17) is used to illustrate the tearing away from old ways. In what areas of your life or faith do you sense God leading you to let go of the old and embrace the new? How can you prepare for this transition?

## LETTER 2

- Reflect on the concept of "burning the plow" as a symbol of complete surrender to God's calling. What are some "plows" in your life—mindsets, roles, or assignments—that you might need to let go of to fully embrace the new season God is leading you into?

- The chapter speaks of two fires—the fire to receive and the fire to conceive. How can you discern which season of refinement you are in? What steps can you take to allow God to work through this process in your life?

- Pioneers often experience seasons of isolation and rejection, even from close relationships. How can you reframe moments of isolation as opportunities for intimacy with God? What biblical promises or truths can sustain you during these challenging times?

## LETTER 3

- Reflect on the concept of picking up the unique mantle God has for you. What are some fears or doubts that might hold you back from embracing your calling? How can you overcome these hesitations?
- The chapter emphasizes the discipline of daily faithfulness over immediate results. How can you remain faithful to your calling even when you don't see immediate fruit? What role does faith play in sustaining your efforts during the "underground" season?
- The chapter speaks of the mantle of "clean hands and a pure heart" (Psalm 24). How can you cultivate purity and holiness in your life to ascend the hill of the Lord? What practical steps can you take to ensure your work remains undefiled and uncompromised?

## LETTER 4

- Reflect on the vision of the "scrolls of destiny" with disjointed, torn, and blank pages. How can you trust God to connect, heal, and fill the chapters of your life that feel unresolved or incomplete? Discuss steps can you take to lean into His guidance during seasons of transition.
- We are co-authors with God in shaping our destiny. How can we actively participate in "rewriting" the story of our lives, especially in areas where we have experienced loss or failure?

- Discuss the process of stepping into new and unknown areas, even when things don't "add up." What risks or leaps of faith is God calling you to take in this season? What do you anticipate as you move ahead?

## LETTER 5

- The chapter uses the imagery of vultures to describe those who prey on your struggles and failures. Who or what in your life might be acting as a "vulture," and how can you discern their true intentions? What steps can you take to set healthy boundaries and protect your focus and future?
- We must leave behind past failures, pain, and stagnation. What are some areas in your life where you may still be "rehearsing the misery of your past"? How can you practically and spiritually step into health and newness?
- Vultures are contrasted with eagles who rise above negativity and focus on their calling. How can you adopt an "eagle mindset" to remain steadfast in your journey? What does the view look like from up there?

## LETTER 6

- You must return to God's original, seemingly impossible vision for your life. What dreams or visions have you adjusted or downsized due to fear or doubt? How can you trust God to help you step into "shoes that are ten sizes too big"?
- Reflect on the story of Nehemiah and the opposition he faced while rebuilding the wall. How can you stay focused and motivated when facing criticism, doubts, or spiritual resistance? Name a few strategies can you use to "stay alert and keep building"?
- The chapter challenges pioneers to build not just for today but for future generations. How can you approach your current

calling with a mindset of legacy and long-term impact? What practical steps can you take to ensure your work lays a foundation for those who come after you?

## LETTER 7

- Reflect on the story of the car sale and the counterfeit offers. How can you develop discernment to recognize "bogus offers" or distractions in your spiritual journey? What practical steps can you take to guard the calling and vision God has placed on your life?
- The chapter warns against settling for less than God's promises by acting out of impatience or fear. In what areas of your life might you be tempted to create an "Ishmael"? How can you wait faithfully for God's timing and provision without losing hope?
- The chapter identifies three areas as battlegrounds for pioneers (positioning, provision, purpose). Which of these areas resonates most with your current situation? How can you align your actions with God's guidance to overcome challenges and step into His plans for you?

## LETTER 8

- We must take back territory that is under the rule of principalities. How does this concept resonate with your personal or spiritual journey? What practical or spiritual steps can you take to reclaim "territory" in your life or community for God's kingdom? What is the result of failing to do so?
- Reflect on the story of Abraham being called to leave his familiar land for a promised territory. What is your promised territory and how can you embrace the uncertainty of the "new land" with faith and trust?

- It's critically important that we see with spiritual vision and continually dream with God. How can you cultivate a spiritually mindset of joyful expectation for your God-dreams? What can happen to someone who neglects dreaming with God?

## LETTER 9

- The letter speaks about the crushing, painful seasons likened to Jesus' Gethsemane experience. What have been some of your own Gethsemane moments, and how did you encounter God in the midst of them? How can you draw strength from these experiences for future challenges?
- The chapter highlights how pressing and crushing produce the "oil" of worship, anointing, and burning for Jesus. How have your own trials refined your character or deepened your relationship with God? What "oil" do you feel God has produced through your journey?
- The letter assures that there is always a breakthrough if you keep walking. How do you maintain hope and perseverance when you're in the middle of a dark or uncertain season? What promises from God can you hold onto during these times?

## LETTER 10

- The chapter describes a shift in language that pioneers experience when God refines and commissions them. Have you noticed changes in how you express your faith or mission? What challenges have you faced in communicating this "new tongue" to others?
- The dream about the bear highlights fear as a major distraction from fulfilling one's calling. What specific fears or distractions have been "chasing" you? Can you recall others who have overcome these same fears? What can you learn from them?

- There is a creative power in language to shape culture, destinies, and movements. What words or messages has God placed on your heart to speak into the world? How can you use your voice to bring His creative and redemptive work to life?

## LETTER 11

- There is a necessary shift from building empires to building families that is happening. Reflect on your current priorities. Are you investing more in outward achievements or in the health and legacy of your family and spiritual community?
- The letter discusses addressing generational dysfunctions and starting a new legacy. Are there cycles in your family or community that need to be broken? What actions can you take to create a new foundation for future generations?
- God calls us to build authentic families, not structures or institutions. In what ways can you foster genuine connections in your home, church, or community? How can you contribute to creating an environment where others feel truly seen and valued?

## LETTER 12

- The vision described pioneers with targets on their backs, often unaware of their spiritual significance. Have you ever felt under attack without understanding why? How might recognizing the spiritual importance of your work help you persevere through challenges?
- Spiritual thresholds often present us with resistance. Are there areas in your life where you feel stuck or blocked? What does it look like to push through these impasses with worship and faith?
- This letter emphasizes that opposition is a natural part of pioneering. How do you usually react to opposition or slander?

How can strategies from the chapter (e.g., worship, staying focused on Jesus, leaning on Scripture) help you to overcome these challenges?

## LETTER 13

- Every Christian must shake off the "mud" and forgive those who have hurt them. What burdens, offenses, or unresolved pain from the past might you need to surrender to God to move forward freely?
- The letter highlights how distraction is often used by the enemy to derail pioneers. Can you identify areas where distraction has taken your focus off God's calling? How can you cultivate discernment to stay aligned with your purpose?
- What fears or hesitations do you face when considering a new season of pioneering, and how can trusting God's promises, like Isaiah 22:22, help you take that first step? Discuss this section of Scripture and how God is speaking to you through it.

## LETTER 14

- Families are prophetic units and called to reveal the heart of the Father. How can you intentionally cultivate an atmosphere in your home that aligns with this calling and fosters God's presence?
- Migration often comes with spiritual warfare and resistance. What are some biblical accounts of trouble-in-transition that you can draw strength from?
- What "dust" from previous seasons do you need to shake off, and how can trusting God's timing help you embrace the new season with faith and joy? How has this practice benefitted you in your journey with Jesus so far? Give specific examples.

## LETTER 15

- David demonstrated boldness and obedience in facing Goliath. What giants—personal or societal—are you being called to confront, and how can you step out in faith, relying on God's strength instead of your own?
- The chapter emphasizes the importance of spiritual weapons over human strategies. How can you shift your focus from natural methods to spiritual tools like prayer, worship, and the Word of God to confront challenges in your life or ministry?
- The imagery of the "five stones" speaks to the unity and activation of the five-fold ministry. How can you contribute to fostering unity and mobilizing the church to rise together against the giants in your community or nation?

## LETTER 16

- The story of hacking through the lantana bush illustrates perseverance. Reflect on a time when you faced a significant obstacle in your own journey. How did you push through, and what lessons did you learn from the experience that might help others who are facing an obstacle of their own?
- Every battle yields spoils. How can you shift your perspective during difficult seasons to focus on the potential rewards and growth God has for you on the other side? Discuss Romans 5:3-5 and how this passage bears these truths.
- The author shares about experiencing God's favor and support after persevering through trials. How have you experienced God showing up in unexpected ways during or after a challenging season? What has "favor and support" looked like in your life, practically speaking?

## LETTER 17

- The chapter highlights the importance of rest and healing for pioneers after prolonged battles. How can you create intentional space in your life to allow God to heal your emotional and spiritual wounds?
- In the vision, Jesus reveals the purpose of the fire as a process of purification and preparation for more. How does this perspective change the way you view seasons of difficulty or "darkroom" moments in your journey?
- The author shares the reminder Jesus gave him, "What makes you think this life is your own?" What are the implications of such a statement for us? What are the consequences of thinking that we are the owners of our lives?

## LETTER 18

- The letter emphasizes the importance of staying true to your unique voice and calling. How can you embrace the way God has uniquely designed you, even when it feels "out of the box" or different from others? How do you combat insecurity in those moments?
- The author shares the importance of not being a "vending machine" for others' spiritual needs. How can you establish healthy boundaries in your ministry or personal life to ensure you remain connected to God without burnout?
- The chapter advises emerging voices to prioritize Jesus, family, and personal health over ministry. What practical steps can you take to maintain this balance in your own life? Can you recall any cautionary tales, where a leader has failed to get this right? What can you learn from it?

## LETTER 19

- We often have to let go of past methods and embrace God's adjustments. What areas in your life or ministry might need surrender or recalibration to align with God's plans? What past methods does God want to reform?
- The "pause" season is presented as preparation for the "go" season. How can you use periods of waiting to seek clarity and strength for the next steps God has for you? What unique challenges come with the "pause" season compared to the "go" season?
- How do the truths in Psalm 32:8 give you comfort and encouragement while carrying out your "marching orders"? Discuss other Psalms and Scriptures you can lean on while going about this next phase for the body of Christ.

## LETTER 20

- The chapter emphasizes surrendering dreams and trusting God for redemption. Are there dreams or promises you've felt were lost that God may be asking you to surrender in faith for His restoration?
- Disappointment and delayed hope can weigh heavily on the heart. How can you lean into God's promise of redemption to move from survival mode into renewed faith and expectation?
- The letter speaks of God bringing things full circle. Have you experienced moments where God has redeemed past pain or disappointment? How can those testimonies fuel your faith for future redemption?

## LETTER 21

- The letter speaks of stepping away from the busyness of life and ministry to prioritize intimacy with God. How can you intentionally create space in your life to ascend the "mountain of the

Lord" and seek His presence more deeply? What are the short-term and long-term benefits of doing so?

- The chapter calls pioneers to rise above spiritual battles fought in the wrong places. What do these "wrong places" look like? What are the benefits of changing the venue, so to speak?
- We have been challenged, as pioneers, to build and speak according to God's direction, even when it appears foolish to others. Can you recall times when God's direction has felt unconventional or misunderstood in your life? How did this play out?

## LETTER 22

- The metaphor of "buying the field" is repeatedly used to describe acts of obedience and faith. How does this metaphor resonate with your understanding of faith and sacrifice? What does "buying the field" mean in your current season of life, and how can you apply this principle today?
- The letter discusses "hallmark of faith moments" as times when obedience and perseverance through trials lead to a visible mark of God's faithfulness. Identify a "hallmark of faith moment" in your life or in the life of someone you admire. How does this moment illustrate the relationship between faith, perseverance, and divine fulfillment?
- According to the chapter, in the months to come you will be stirred in ways you have not felt in years. What practical steps can you take to steward this stirring? Discuss some of the results you anticipate as you yield to this new work of the Lord.

Made in the USA
Columbia, SC
19 March 2025

55392610R00148